The Stories

A Journey through Time

with William Charles Light

ISBN 0-9778788-0-5
ISBN13 978-0-9778788-0-2

LIGHT INNOVATIVE CONCEPTS LCC
SAN 850-4997
Greenville, Ohio

COVER

Artist Tom Triplett and the author created the cover graphic jointly. It is a characterization of the author in his "Flim Flam Man" regalia. Throughout their lives, the author and his family participated together in many activities, and a favorite pastime was "Rendezvous" where black powder muzzleloader shooters got together to relive an interesting and exciting time in America's past. We continue traditional skills and crafts at these events, including the telling of stories. The graphic shows the Flim Flam Man holding a crystal ball that contains a 1950's view of his brothers and him. The cover and other art in this book accurately reflect vignettes contained within the stories.

I dedicate this book to my loving family, and thank them for their understanding and patience that allowed me to enjoy so many side roads in life's wonderful journey.

I also want to express my sincere appreciation for the delightful artwork created by my good friend and loyal student, Tom Triplett, who created several of the illustrations in this book.

Last, but surely not least, many thanks to classmate and personal editor Chuck Devor for keeping my English honest.

Table of Contents

Introduction:

For many years, the stories have surfaced in my head like a dolphin bobbing up among the ocean waves following a deep and lengthy feeding dive. The brief narratives have formed colorful vignettes, feeding my soul and on many occasions keeping my mind from sinking into the depths of self-pity and despair.

Over my 50-plus years of survival on this yo-yo orb of kindness, hatred, love, war, peace, friendships, enemies, work, recreation, family, loneliness, feast and famine, it has been the stories that have kept me afloat in this curious sea of life and near death.. The stories have formed at unexpected points in time along the journey. Through the years, they have aged like a fine German wine, although many, when opened to a crowd of first-time listeners, sound more like a boisterous German beer party. The gift of the stories is in the telling - currents of knowledge and myth that sputter through the river of life. They flood and trickle, but always they revive forces that remove present-day boulders from my path along the journey.

From childhood in an 85-neighbor, Ohio village to the present, my family and I have retold the stories for insiders and outsiders. The stories have extended my immediate family by absorbing those who have listened. They are a vehicle that has carried life lessons, knowledge and emotions into the future. They are the ribbons that bond a community together and give it purpose.

The thought of recording the stories for all to see always seemed such a daunting task. However, the possibility of merely reading a story seemed to risk losing the very soul of the story. You see: the art of the story is in the telling. A grizzly bear story means much more when your nostrils are filling with campfire smoke in a dark Michigan forest and a falling twig sounds precisely like the stalking footstep of the great beast. Then, the unexpected scream of an older brother sends shivers up your spine as your mind sees him dragged away from camp by the hairy brute. It also helps when the storyteller is wearing a four-day growth of gray-tinted red hair on his face. A collective laughter circles the fire and breaks the tension, and then the story continues.

"Can the stories be told effectively without the appropriate environment and audience?" I have pondered. "What about those wonderfully-colorful persons about whom the stories are told? Would they recognize themselves, regardless of the false names and locations given them, and be insulted?" This would not be tolerable, for the stories are not about demeaning; they are about acceptance into the broad community of life.

Perhaps a risk greater than loss of color or possible insult is the stories are lost forever. As our family structures continue to erode under the constant strain of "social improvement," and humanity continues to become more isolated as it is crowded, like rats into ever-growing urban centers, it is apparent that the art of the story and its telling may not survive. It was only this realization that has caused me to come out of my writing hibernation and attempt to jot down a collection of real-life, "honest-to-God" stories onto the printed page. It is my grand faith in the imagination of the individual that gives me the strength to imagine that this collection might help keep the art alive.

With these thoughts in mind, it is time to see, listen and feel snippets in the times and lives of fellow human beings along their life journeys. Each **COLLECTION** of stories is provided with a **CANVAS** upon which the setting, its surroundings and atmosphere will be painted to help your mind settle into a mood receptive to the **STORIES**. The stories are organized by **CHAPTERS** within each collection. Each story has a **TITLE** and may or may not be bracketed by commentary. It is best to read each story in order to maintain the thread of the canvas.

Perhaps you may wish to pass the stories on to your family or friends. Better yet, use this book to help remind you of the stories in your past. Let the journey begin.

Collection #1:

Canvas: Fort Jefferson – Home on the Hill

Setting: 1946-1965, a very small rural Ohio village with a shrinking population of about 85 humans and a cadre of so-called domesticated animals and numerous wild ones. It was a tree-covered historical landmark. It boasted its own state park that occupied about one-fourth of village landmass. Small farms surrounded the community.

The village sat on a gentle hill at the intersection of a state highway and a county road, and it had two general stores. It had no government; however, it contained the Neave Township building, which looked and felt more like a Quaker meeting hall, including a few hard, wooden church pews and an elevated section of floor where township officials lifted themselves above the "masses." People voted here and Boy Scouts held sacred rituals during winter meetings and planned great, summertime outdoor adventures.

A Methodist church sat on the highest point at the northwest corner of the community along side of its ancient cemetery. The "modern" cemetery sat atop another small hill located about 300-yards south of the village. Fort Jefferson was a supply fort for historic Fort Greenville, located about five miles to the north. Greenville was the home of such dignitaries as "Little Sure Shot" Annie Oakley, famous news broadcaster Lowell Thomas, telescope manufacturers The Lohmann Brothers and dirigible pilot Zachary Landsdowne. Greenville seemed like a metropolis to Jeffersonites (because we had no famous folks) and most of us made weekly pilgrimages there.

Fort Jefferson's only school, located another 300 yards south, was later consolidated with other surrounding schools; a single school bus stop carted us north to Greenville or south to New Madison, another frontier community, formerly Fort Black.

To the west of Ft. Jefferson sat one of the country's first conservation initiatives called Wayne Lakes Park. For numerous years, American Aggregates, a gravel conglomerate, mined the aggregates created by the great glacier during the last ice age, and then converted the series of deep and oddly shaped pits into clean, spring-fed lakes. My grandfather, a former newspaper owner, managed this park and its fish hatchery, and it kept him busy during his "retirement" years. More people lived here, scattered around the lakes in small cottages, than lived in Ft. Jefferson.

Our 200-year old house sat on a one-acre lot at the southeast corner of the intersecting state highway and the county road. The house was a two and one-half story timber frame building with 17-inch, hand-hewn wall plates and half-round logs for floor joists. There is a rock-walled basement under the north half of the building. The old building started life as a roadside inn that was constructed after the fort was burned to the ground. When first built, it was much larger as it stretched to the south property line and then took a left hand turn, extending back to a two-track, gravel driveway that stretched along our eastern border. An abandoned tunnel ran from the old fort to a prairie located about 300 yards down the hill and east of our house. Its wall ran within inches of the south foundation of the house.

The "Homestead," as we called it, was solid, and three large trees flanked it on two sides. A black walnut tree and a large maple tree stood directly out the back door while another walnut tree clung to life along a small rock wall that bordered the alleyway and merged as a foundation for our two-car garage that never held a car, except when one needed repair. A small woodshed that occasionally was converted to the Light Brothers Clubhouse, sat directly south of the garage.

It was a quiet community with a normal distribution of young, middle aged and old folks. Neighbors still knew one another.

Chapter #1: Buddy's Stories

Knowing what I know today, if God would grant me the opportunity to be born again into the world, without question I would choose Fort Jefferson, Ohio. My one stipulation would be that I really would want to be born retaining exactly what I know today.

My father used to say we were a blessed community because, "most towns this size have only one village idiot, but we have two." I am not sure, but at times, I think he was referring to me. Don't get the wrong idea here. Dad was one of the least judgmental men I have ever met. Moreover, he was right! Fort Jefferson did have its fair share of folks who would be judged intellectually lacking under most standards. What is most important here is that we were a community, a place where people were accepted for what they were or chose to be and where they were encouraged to be more. For example, there was Guy Budmeier.

Guy was raised in a "rough" family and, by today's politically correct society, would be called mentally challenged (a sad testament to today's society). It was the outsiders who looked down upon Guy from their "all-knowing" perches. They just knew he was disadvantaged and needed their infinite wisdom to survive. We just called Guy, "Buddy," and he was who he was. Buddy stuttered rather dramatically when he talked. Buddy started grade school with my mother and was proud when he announced to Mom's father, "I sta-sta-started to sca-sca-school wa-wa-wa-with Ar-Arline and buh-buh-buh-bygollie today La-La-La-Lillian wa-wa-went ah-ah-around me." Lillian was Mom's younger sister by five years. Buddy never finished school, but he was always proud of those who did, including all three of his children. During my childhood, I found Buddy to be one of the most loving and caring people I had ever known. He married and had several children. In fact, even though Buddy was considered mentally slow, he single-handedly built the family house in which he lived for the remainder of his life. Not only did he build his own house, but also, in my mind, he was a great educator. Let me explain. To this very day, I use knowledge gained from Buddy to train fellow engineers. The story speaks of this knowledge that is engraved in my brain so deeply that Alzheimer's will have a hard time rubbing it out.

Story #1: Lesson Learned

It was a very hot and humid day in southwestern Ohio as Buddy tied up his nail apron, sheathed his hammer and climbed the wobbly wooden ladder that was resting precariously on the eave of the old church.

"Da-da-da-da-damn hot da-da-day a-a-a-a-ain't it," Buddy stuttered to his fellow workers as he reached the edge of the metal lapped roofing. Buddy was prone to use a few colorful expressions when he spoke, even if it was a church roof, but don't confuse this with a lack of faith. Buddy was a God-fearing Methodist and a regular at Sunday services on the hill.

Buddy and his fellow workers were

fixing leaks at the peak of the standing-seam roofing. The temperature had climbed to about 92 degrees and heat waves could be seen radiating from the shiny surface. Buddy, one of the strongest individuals I have ever met, became thirsty and decided to rise to his feet to fetch a cup of water. "Tha-tha-tha-think I-I-I-I'll ga-ga-ga-ga-get a ta-ta-ta-taste of wa-wa-wa-water," he shouted as he turned to walk. Suddenly, Buddy's feet kicked out from under him and he landed flat on his back, zipping down the silvery slide at breakneck speed. He had only seconds to make a life-or-death decision before plunging over the edge and diving three stories to the ground, or more precisely to a cluttered concrete apron.

Now put yourself in Buddy's shoes. By the time you read this sentence, you will have flown wildly over the brink. Too late! And, you are supposedly bright and educated. Obviously, Buddy did not fly off the edge or I probably would not be telling this story. Moreover, God did not reach down and lend a helping hand. As stated earlier, these are true, honest-to-God stories. How Buddy saved his life probably wasn't repeated openly at the church social, but in the hallways, it was the topic of the day. As Buddy was rapidly gaining speed on his death slide, he swiftly reached down with both hands and yanked his denim work pants and underwear to his folded knees, exposing his pale butt cheeks to the hot metal surface. With a subtle "eek...eek" sound, Buddy came to a sudden stop. Without a word spoken, Buddy regained his footing, pulled up his pants, got a cup of water, spit one mouthful over the edge for good measure, pulled a gooey handkerchief from his rear pocket and blew his nose, then promptly returned to the roof peak.

The lesson to be learned here is not, "How can I prevent myself from sliding off a hot, standing-seam metal roof?" The real lesson is not to judge people by how you perceive their intelligence, but rather to accept them for their unique wisdom and heart. Buddy had a lot of heart. Buddy loved his children and was very protective of them. Nevertheless, as with all parenting, sometimes things do not go as planned and sometimes we just get lucky. Such was the case with Buddy in our next story.

Story #2: Timing is Everything

Mid-summer had arrived and as a 12-year-old on summer vacation in a small town, I was looking for something to do – anything. I could have pulled out my flippin' pole and headed for the creek for a relaxing day of bluegill fishing; or in this case, I decided to do something more exciting – to check on Buddy as he constructed his new home next to Bakker's Orchard. Buddy sometimes worked doing odd jobs for the Bakkers, but not today. He was putting the roof up on his new house, hoping to move his family out of his mother's home, sooner than later.

As I headed up the grass-filled alley, I could hear the persistent banging of Buddy's hammer. The hammering stopped as I approached the topless house, and as I scanned the yard like an army intelligence officer, I noticed Buddy's three children, Connie, Heady and Timmy, playing in the yard below the developing structure. As I raised my eyes skyward, I saw Buddy wrestling a large roofing plank. Without warning, he flung the plank, with all his massive strength, into the air. Like a missile, the 12-

foot plank hurled towards the unsuspecting children below. At that same instant, Buddy panicked as he spotted the children. "Ka-Ka-Ka-Ka-Ka-Ka-Ka-Ka-Connie!" he shouted, "Ga-Ga-Ga-Ga-Ga-Ga-Get ya-ya-ya-your ska-ska-ska-ska-ska-skinny a-a-a-a-ass out of the wa-wa-wa-wa-wa-way!" Of course, the board had reached the ground (uneventfully) several seconds before Buddy could shout out the warning.

-30-

I told my grandmother this story when I reached home. She said, "God protects the unfortunate." I had never thought of Buddy being unfortunate. In fact, I looked up to him. He was stronger than any man I had ever met. Moreover, I learned lots of words and phrases I never heard around our house. Take the phrase "skinny ass" for example. It is a very descriptive phrase and one of Buddy's favorites. He used it frequently and quite openly, even around strangers who did not think it was a proper phrase to use around proper children. Dad never seemed to mind Buddy's choice of words. However, he did seem somewhat upset when I would use them. Occasionally, most likely motivated by my mother, he would say something like, "As you get smarter, perhaps you can use words of greater length than just four letters." Over time, I learned to separate the different worlds, but I always enjoyed Buddy's language, and I learned it well.

Story #3: Wild Animals in the Woodshed

When the Light family moved to America in the 1690's, it was a skilled-trades family. Due to various marriages and the like, and by the time it came time for my generation, several branches of the family were gun makers. My father was a research hydraulic engineer for experimental aircraft, but at home, he was a gunsmith at heart. Consequently, every corner of our house was filled with firearms of all shapes and sizes. Many firearms stacked here and about seemed very natural to me. My brothers and I learned early in life to respect both guns and our parents' directives. Now the reason for this sidebar is to allow you to understand how the family was perceived in Fort Jefferson. Dad was perceived something like Matt Dillon of the TV series, "Gun Smoke." It was fitting because Dad was always a peacemaker. Dad and Mick Mong, who owned the general store across the state highway, would every so often decide which one would be the Mayor and which would be the Chamber of Commerce president. This was necessary because Dutch, the mail carrier, had to know where to deliver the letters addressed to these positions. If you recall, Fort Jefferson does have a one-acre state park.

One night as our family huddled around the small television screen watching "I Love Lucy," there came a frantic pounding at our door. It was a wild-eyed Buddy. Buddy never knocked. He always pounded, but this pounding hammered out an urgency that was unusual. Dad opened the door and was greeted with Buddy shouting, "Ja-ja-ja-ja-James! Th-there's ah-ah-ah-ah- wa-wa-wa-wawild a-a-a-a-animal i-i-i-i-in muh-muh-my wooooooood sha-sha-shed. Ka-ka-ka-come ka-ka-ka-ka-quick. It ma-ma-ma-made a terrible na-na-na-na-noise!"

Dad pulled a rifle from a kitchen wall corner and grabbed a few rounds, and out the door we went – all three brothers, Dad and Buddy.

Now, I know I told you that Buddy was the strongest man I had ever met. However, understand strength does not necessarily eliminate fear. Buddy had his share of fear, especially when it came to "wild animals in the woodshed." When our armed camp arrived at the woodshed, it was a scary moment. I have no idea what my brothers were thinking, but in my mind I knew that when the door was opened, Dad would be charged by a black panther that had escaped from some zoo 80 miles away. Dad, on the other hand, seemed to have no fear. I could not understand why, especially since Buddy had already explained that it was a "wild animal." Most of the animals around Fort Jefferson were not wild, so it had to be some evil intruder.

The time came for the great door opening. Buddy's three kids had arrived on the scene and it was a remarkable sight. All six kids were pushing closer and closer to the woodshed, while Dad started to open the door. Suddenly, Buddy shouted, "Ka-Ka-Ka-Ka-Ka-Ka-Ka-Ka-Connie! Ga-

ga-ga-get ya-ya-ya-your ska-ska-ska-ska-skinny a-a-a-a-a-ass out of the way 'fore it ee-ee-ee-ee-eats ya allllll up." We all quickly backed up several paces as the door squeaked open. The tension mounted as Buddy shined his flashlight into the black abyss of the shed. The beam nervously moved back and forth, but no lion, tiger or buffalo was to be seen. "Maybe it had left the scene and is lurking behind us," I worried. Dad casually took the flashlight, knelt down and lifted up a loose board. An eerie hissing noise emitted from under the board, and all six children shuttled back a few more yards.

The flashlight suddenly illuminated a mother possum with her litter of small possums. We all breathed a sigh of relief as Dad explained to all that the animal was harmless and most likely would not "eat us all up." No shots were fired and mother possum and kids were left to be a permanent family in our fine village.

-30-

To understand Buddy is to have a better understanding of life. If you, like some of my more left-of-center friends, have assumed that he was a poor, unassuming unfortunate fellow, you would be wrong. He was a respected man in our community. He had a good heart, a wonderful soul and a great temper. He is in good company because it is my understanding that God possesses these same characteristics. Buddy always stood up for his family and his family's rights, and my next story exemplifies this fact.

Story #4: The Sears and Roebuck Wrench

The leaves were falling on this bright fall afternoon as I meandered through Claude and Summy Shaffer's garden. They owned the general store that sat across the county road from our 200-year-old home. Claude and Summy had migrated from West Virginia to Fort Jefferson when Claude developed back problems from working the coalmines. The illness kept Claude in a permanent 90-degree bend at the waist, unless he could push himself up by placing his hands on the countertop. The store and household were one, with the latter located in the rear of the store and separated by only a shabby cloth curtain. As a very young child, I remember seeing Summy standing vertically, but mostly I remember her being confined to a wheel chair where she remained for the rest of her life. It did not matter, though, as Claude and Summy were like a second set of parents for us boys. It was not unusual for us to gather around their small television and watch professional wrestling. Don Eagle was my favorite, but to Claude and Summy, this was a serious event and they watched with great fervor. Yelling and screaming was quite acceptable whether customers were present or not.

Now, I have taken you to this store because it was the town gathering point. Mick Mong's store, located diagonally across the intersection was more formal and served only as a shopping place and cold-weather stop for kids waiting for the school bus in winter. The Shaffer's' store was a little shabby, but a lot more homey. It had rough wooden floors, a few throw rugs and a large potbellied stove that was centrally located. The stove had a foot ring that surrounded it, as did an assortment of seven chairs. Townsfolk and farmers would gather here at all times of the day and evenings. Both stores had two gas pumps in front. They were way ahead of their times because everyone self-served themselves to the gasoline.

Occasionally, the potbellied stove was a place of excitement. Take the day when Shorty Longfellow walked in and wanted a seat around the stove. Local farmers filled the chairs. They felt no obligation to give up a warm seat on a cold winter day. Now, you must understand that Shorty was not only a farmer but he was also the main dynamite salesman for Darke County. Shorty casually left the store, walked to his truck, pulled out a stick of dynamite, then quietly reentered the establishment and headed for the stove. Without a word, he waved the dynamite in the air, opened the stove door and then tossed it in. There was a great disruption as all the farmers fled the building. Shorty calmly took a seat and propped his feet up for a few minutes rest. Most folks don't know that dynamite takes both percussion and heat to make it explode, but Shorty did! It was a day that will live in infamy.

Well, back to my story. As I walked through the garden, I saw Claude bent over raking leaves and that meant that Summy was in the store alone. Summy was tight with a buck when Claude was in sight, and she pretty much ran the store. However, when alone, she tended to hand out candy to wondering waifs like me. I headed for the store and, sure enough, got my sugar fix. I was sitting in front of the television when Buddy walked in. He talked with Summy a few minutes and in this conversation, I heard Buddy say that he was working on his Plymouth. I had never seen Buddy work on a car engine before, so I followed him back to his house, and as announced in Summy's store, the hood was up on his rusting auto. Buddy picked up a fine 3/4-inch Craftsman end wrench from his toolbox, placed the wrench on one of the engine nuts and began to twist. Apparently, the nut was rusted fast so Buddy began to add a little more energy to his effort. The next few sounds were new to me. It sounded something like, "Pink, thump sha-sha-sha-shit." I had never seen anyone snap a 3/4"-inch Craftsman end wrench into two pieces simply by hand power. It bolstered my belief that Buddy was the strongest man in the world and that he, most likely, could whip Don Eagle.

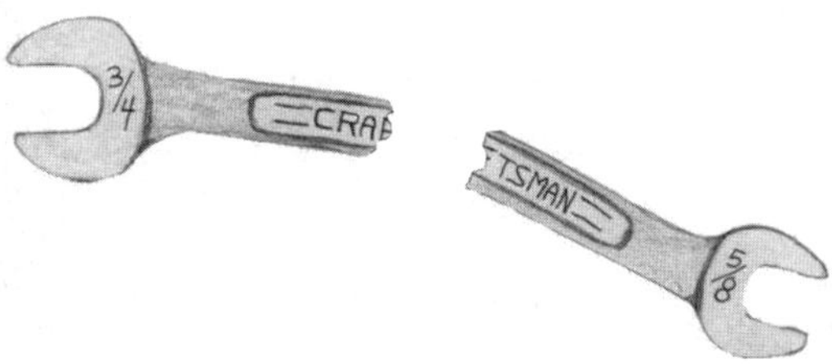

The remainder of this story came to the Light household via the manager of the Sears and Roebuck store located in Greenville. You see, Sears and Roebuck sold Craftsman tools exclusively and these tools carried a lifetime guarantee against breakage. In fact, that was the very reason Buddy had bought the Craftsman wrench. Buddy packed up his two-piece wrench and headed to Greenville in a borrowed car. Upon arrival at the store a rather short and cocky salesman, who was known for making snide remarks, greeted Buddy at the counter. Buddy handed the man the broken tool and simply stated, "I I I ba-ba-ba-broke ma-ma-ma-my ra-ra-ra-wrench." The salesman slid the pieces across the counter, squinted, then looked up at buddy and sneered, "What'd ya do, run over it with a truck?"

Buddy's immediate response was quickly to reach across the counter with both hands, firmly grasp the salesman's suit coat lapels, and then yank the salesman across the counter for an eyeball-to-eyeball conversation. Buddy replied, "Heh-heh-heh-hell no, I ya-ya-used a ta-tank!" At that moment, the store manager arrived on the scene and convinced Buddy that the store would stand behind its products and promptly provided him with a new 3/4-inch Craftsman end wrench, which he owned to his death.

My last visit with Buddy occurred in the late 1960's when I visited my parents and Buddy was busily painting the overhanging eaves on the third story of the old house. He spent much of the day at the top of the ladder, leaning over backwards and reaching back to paint the large overhang. He came down only to move the ladder a few feet at a time. On one such journey to the bottom of the ladder, he looked at my father and said, "Jeh.Jeh.James. I I I meh-meh-meh-must ba-ba-ba-be getting eh-eh-old. La-la-la-losin' ma-ma-ma-ma-my peh-puff." The job he was doing would have killed younger men. It's a sad memory for me, for it was later learned that Buddy had lung cancer, and the disease eventually claimed his life. Buddy is missed, but will long be remembered and honored in the stories.

Chapter #2: General George

He was a rare spirit. It was known early on in his life that he would have a hard time adjusting to the rapidly changing society of America, but he made it despite his handicaps. His brother and sister were bright and energetic and his father and mother were hard-workers. George was slow on wit and intellect, but some of his stories might teach you the life lessons I learned.

Story #5: Grandpa Died

Mom always was a magnet for wayward youths and that Thursday morning was no exception. It wasn't that George said anything. It was just the way he was sitting on our concrete walk that alerted Mom that something was not right in George's world.

George sat very still. His shoulders were stooped, and he gazed into space as if seeking some answer that just would not come into his vision. Mom noticed George when she looked out the kitchen window, and she new it was time for a talk. Mom brushed aside the rear screen door and knelt beside George.

"Is something wrong, George?" Mom asked.

"Grandpa died," he responded. Mom hadn't heard the news.

"Which one?" she queried.

After a brief pause, George replied, "The one that married grandma."

-30-

Was it Mom's question or George's answer in errs? There is something poignant within all human minds. There is always knowledge to learn from interaction with fellow human beings, regardless of social status or intellect.

George was raised in a small shack that sat on the south edge of town. In some areas, the floor was dirt. The walls were thin and the space cramped. There were those, even some village residents, who looked down on George and his family. It was their loss. As George grew older, he knew he could not keep pace with the other children as he fell farther and farther behind in school. Finally, he was removed from the school system. George loved to travel and in his youth, his primary mode of transportation was the bicycle that

he painted a new color almost every week. As he approached puberty he wanted to drive cars like everyone else his age, but he could not get a license because he could not read. In fact, George could not remember which was his left or right hand. However, as he acquired menial jobs at local farms and businesses, he needed a manner of transport. For the short hops, he relied on his trusty bicycles, but on longer jaunts, he used a small farm tractor, which he also occasionally painted with bright colors.

One morning at the breakfast table at our house, Dad, without warning, said, "You know, I think George is one of the best mechanics I know." We children, knowing George's limitations, thought it was an odd statement. It wasn't said with humor. There actually was seriousness in his tone of voice. Brother Bob noticed George's bright orange tractor parked in Claude and Summy's parking lot. About that time, George walked out of the store, approached the tractor, reached into a toolbox mounted behind the lone seat, pulled out a hammer and applied three raps to the side of the engine. He placed the hammer back into the toolbox, pushed the start button with his foot and the tractor engine chugged to life with no argument. Dad commented, "See, he only needs one tool." We all nodded and returned to our breakfast.

Story #6: Smoke Gets In Your Eyes

It was one of those sneaky days you sometimes have as a kid. A time for experimentation with smoking ragweed stocks, seeing how fast black powder will burn or perhaps getting into a walnut war with the village archrivals. However, this day was special. George called a meeting in a local burned-out shed across the way. There were only four of us who showed up, including George. Three of us were about 12 years of age while George was 20-something.

We always carried unspoken fear into any meeting with George. As it always turned out, there was no reason to fear. Despite his menacing demeanor and coarse language, George was not spiteful or harmful. George, like most people, strived for excellence and was proud when he achieved a new level of performance, and that was the reason he called the meeting. My other allies and I congregated together before heading for the roofless shed.

"What's up with George?" Kenny asked.

"Damned if I know," Craig replied.

I always talked too much, but I didn't have a clue so I remained quiet as we approached the den of iniquity. George was awaiting our arrival. We took a quick look around, entered, and then closed the double swinging doors.

"What goes?" I questioned.

"I can make smoke come out my eyes," George responded.

"Yeah, right!" says Kenny.

We all laughed, but George remained serious and lighted up a Camel. He took a few puffs on the cigarette and stated, "Watch this."

As God as my witness, what I am about to divulge is true. We three musketeers watched in solemn amazement as George inhaled about 1/4 of the cigarette and then made a strange face that implied that internal pressures were

building somewhere in the bowels of his body. His face turned a fire engine red, his head arched forward and his eyes squeezed so tight that his eyebrows were next to his cheekbones. Suddenly, his head arched up and his eyes opened wide. There it was! Coming out of his lower eyelids were two faint columns of white smoke.

"My God," I thought, "this cannot be real." Nevertheless, it was real, and it continued for about 15 or 20 seconds. It was hard to tell because time seems to stop when you witness something like this. We actually cheered and applauded when George returned from his trance and took a breath of stale air.

-30-

For a small town a miracle like this is a rare thing. As a sheltered child, you are at a loss how to handle such knowledge. My uncle was a veterinarian, but I sincerely doubted that even he would have such knowledge. I wanted to tell the world, but what would be thought of me if parents and neighbors knew that I was studying the science of smoking? What if they learned about my ragweed puffing adventure? Surely, I would be at least ostracized from the family or perhaps sent to reform school at worst.

Uncle Dick the Vet

Within a week or two following the smoking revelation, I mustered the courage to talk with my Uncle Dick about the miracle I had witnessed. In later life, Uncle Dick became more of a brother than an uncle. I had a special relationship with him, so a sensitive discussion about the paranormal was normal. Dick went into great detail explaining that there are tear ducts in the eyes and they connect with the sinus system. He said that what I saw was no miracle, just a demonstration of human will and body control. How disappointing.

From today's perspective, I see that without George I may never have learned about tear ducts and the sinus systems. Moreover, I may never have gotten as close to Uncle Dick as I did.

Story #7: Wanna See Grandpa's Saword

In my formative years, I was a cowboy. I don't mean I worked the range or anything. I just mentally lived and breathed the life of a cowboy. When Uncle Dick moved to a small farm from which to operate his veterinary clinic, he added ponies and horses. Life was getting great.

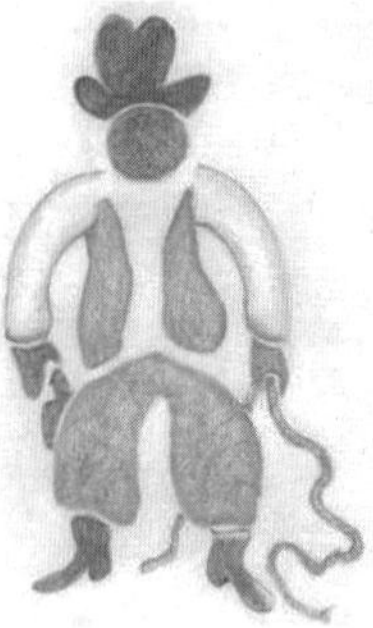

It should be of no surprise when I tell you that I just had to have the twin-holstered cap guns that showed up at Mick Mong's general store. The real ones at our house were not playthings. Consequently, I drooled when I first noticed the cellophane-sealed box sitting conspicuously on the store shelf. Ten dollars was a lot of money for a six-year-old boy in 1953, but God gave me a vision that those guns would be mine. Well, maybe not, but I sure thought He should have.

General George always seemed to have some money when I saw him at Claude and Summy's store, so he seemed to me like the right maple tree to tap. But, how? Then it came to me like a vision. I had an old metal-jacketed desk radio that worked quite well, and I was sure George didn't. So, I trudged down to George's shack with radio in tow. I knew that God was on my side when George agreed to give me ten bucks - exactly what I needed.

I quite literally sprinted back to the store, wrenched the box from the shelf and walked to the cash register where Mick's wife, Stella, was waiting. She rang up the total, and I was suddenly the proud owner of the most wonderful weapons owned by a six-year-old cowboy.

Now it never crossed my mind that someone in the family might ask how I happened to acquire these fine weapons. But, Dad did.

"I bought them at Mick's," I said.

"And, how did you pay for them?" he questioned.

"With ten dollars," I countered.

"And where did you get ten dollars?" he pursued.

I thought I was holding my own up to this point, but I was running out of room fast.

"I sold some stuff," I stalled.

"Just what kind of stuff?" he pried.

"Just some old stuff I don't use anymore," I sweated.

"Specifically, what old stuff?" he pressed.

Dad was a very good debater. I learned this early in life, but for some reason I always felt like I had a chance. This was no exception, so the duel continued.

"Uh, an old, old radio that wasn't good anymore," I admitted.

"And, to whom did you sell the old, old radio?" he twisted.

Some way I just intuitively knew that I had done something wrong, but for the life of me I could not figure out what it was. In fact, it crossed my mind that I might make a good salesman. I figured if I could stall long enough, Dad would give up or I would figure out what I had done wrong. Whichever way it went, I just knew that the question would eventually be answered.

"A good friend," I said softly.

"And, just exactly what good friend would that be?" he persisted.

Well, it wasn't as if I had a 100 or so good friends, so I thought Dad might just assume one of them. He didn't.

Dad repeated, "And, just exactly what good friend would that be?"

"Oh well, I might as well pull the lever to the gallows," I thought. I instinctively knew that I had reached the end of my rope. "George," was my last word as I awaited the doors to be opened beneath my feet.

"Well young man," he sternly started, "You know good and well that George doesn't understand such things as the value of money."

Well, I hadn't known that right up until that moment, but I was never a slow learner when it came from a teacher like Dad. He never had to spank you. His steely gaze could just look you under the table.

"Here's what you are going to do," he continued. "You are going to take those guns back to Mick's; then you are going to take that money back to George. And, you are going to allow George to keep that old, old radio."

It could have been

worse, but alas, at the time I didn't see how. However, as I saw it, I didn't have much choice. So, I followed the sad instructions as demanded.

If this seems like the end of the story, it is not. What happened next was another life lesson for me. I returned the guns to Mick's and ever so slowly started the long journey to the south end of town to return the ten dollars. As I approached the shack, I still mourned the loss of the magnificent cap guns and even considered other ways I could raise the money and perhaps keep the guns under wraps. When I knocked at the door, George answered.

"What's up?" George asked.

"Dad says I gotta give you back this money 'cause the radio isn't worth that much. Oh yeah, you can keep the radio. I don't need it any more."

George accepted the money as if he didn't feel the world shift on its axis as I did. He then surprised me by asking, "Would ya like to see my grandpa's 'saword'?"

I knew what a "sword" was, but I wasn't sure about a "saword."

"Sure," I said, and the two of us walked down the narrow hallway and made a left turn into George's bedroom. It was a cluttered little room and right there on a shelf was my old desk radio, except it was no longer brown. It had been painted a bright green.

As I turned around, I looked up to see hanging on the wall, the most beautiful Civil War cutlass I had ever seen in my life. George pulled the "saword" from its mooring and handed it to me to examine. As I removed the

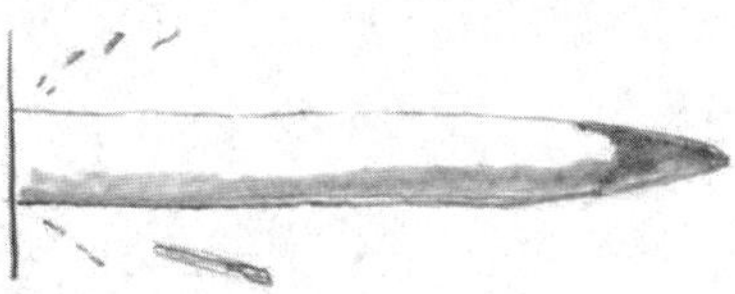

"saword" from the decorative sheath, I asked, "Where did you get this thing?"

"It was grandpa's saword. He was in a war," he said. At that time, George lifted the sword from my arms and casually commented, "And, it's sharp too." Following these words, he plunged the sword through his bedroom wall. For some reason this seemed somewhat normal as I stood in George's bedroom, but somehow I knew that this probably would not be proper conduct at my house. I walked home that night with many of life's mysteries to solve.

-30-

At this juncture, you are probably asking yourself, "If George couldn't read and write, and he didn't know his left from his right hand, how did he ever get the nickname of General George." I thought you would never ask, but I'm glad you did because it makes the perfect segue to my next story. In the next saga, you will learn about the depth of human kindness and that it's okay to laugh with one another, regardless of life station, as long as the spirit is right.

Story #8: Rock Face

As George aged, it became the concern of the community that it would be hard to keep him gainfully employed, especially with the ongoing, fast-paced changes regarding the needs of the workforce. Towards that end, it was thought perhaps that George might find a place in the Ohio National Guard. Even if I knew, I would not tell you how George was helped to find his way into the official roster of the Greenville Post of the Ohio National Guard, but he did. He was a good and enthusiastic worker, but when various inspections and testing occurred, George miraculously passed, almost as if someone else were filling in the answers.

All was going well until the Greenville warriors had to attend the annual pilgrimage to Camp Perry where all of the Ohio National Guard posts came to train and compete. What was the post commander to do? The marching competition was very strict and each post had to march all of its members. Having George feign sickness was out of the question as George was not a good actor. George could march okay, but when the commander would bark, "Right face!" George was just as likely to turn left. George did just fine with about face, halt and forward march, but left and right were out of the question.

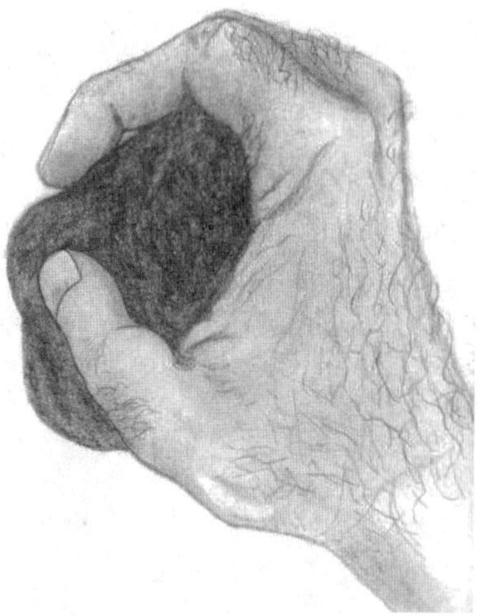

What's a mother to do? As the troops lined up for the marching competition, the post commander came up with a stroke of genius. He reached down and picked up a smooth, round stone from the roadbed. He walked up to George, grabbed George's right arm, and then planted the stone firmly in George's right palm.

"George," the commander said firmly, "when I bark, 'Rock face' you turn towards the rock I just placed in your right hand. If I say, 'Left face,' you turn the other way."

George nodded, and off they went, straight into the marching competition.

Now I know that as you hear my stories, you think they are full of exaggeration. They are not, and the records of the Ohio National Guard will verify what happened next. For the first time in the history of the Greenville Post, it won the marching competition at Camp Perry. George performed flawlessly. It came time for the Greenville post to accept its award; the troops were called to attention and started marching towards the review stand to collect the trophy. On the way to the stand the post commander shouted, "Rock face!" and George immediately turned left and crashed into some of his fellow marchers. He scrambled back in line and continued to the reviewing stand. As the troops marched back towards the tents, the post commander dropped back to see George and asked, "What happened George?"

George's simple but honest reply was, "Dropped that God-damn stone."

So what does all that have to do with the nickname General George? Unfortunately, after this all-time high, George was preparing to clean his rifle while sitting in his tent. The rifle was loaded and the weapon accidentally discharged, shooting a hole through a nearby general's tent while the general was still sitting in it. So ended the military career of General George, who left the National Guard with a well-deserved honorable discharge.

Story #9: Swinging Beauty

Several years later, I returned to Fort Jefferson from my Michigan home for a family reunion. Dad and brothers were sitting in the living room watching football when Dad, who had glanced out the front window, said, "What on earth?" Immediately, we sons jumped from our chairs and looked. There was George riding his bicycle while suspending a large eight-foot long, twelve-inch wide plank of wood under his arm. We all watched in amazement as George rode up to a house located diagonally across the street and dropped the plank. He then sped away back towards his house. What we failed to notice, at first, was the young lady (about George's age) that was swinging back and forth upon a porch swing. She was new to the village but seemed content with her swinging.

We had no sooner slipped back into our chairs than Dad said, "Oh boy." It was back to the window for more spying. This time George was toting a concrete block under his arm. He reached Swinging Beauty's sidewalk and placed the block under one end of the plank. George rode his bike back several yards, turned and addressed the newly manufactured ramp and took a deep breath. He then pedaled with all of his might and launched himself and the bicycle into the air. Swinging Beauty was obviously impressed with the private thrill show and showed her appreciation with a wide smile. George made several more daring passes, but Swinging Beauty seemed to lose interest, as did we, so we returned to our chairs.

"For heaven's sake," was Dad's next provocation to force us to relinquish our seats. This time we saw George carrying another concrete block past our window. He raised the risk stakes and hopefully Swinging Beauty's affection, two times higher. Repeatedly he ramped over the precipice with grace and vigor. Once more Swinging Beauty was openly impressed for a short period, but alas, her fickle female heart waned. George left and we left our window to go back to football. We thought the private show was over until Dad gasped, "Oh, my God!" Much to our horror we could only watch as George doused the homemade thrill show ramp with gasoline and ignited it. With added determination George and his bicycle charged the flaming launch with tremendous speed and the flames parted as he shot free from the earthly bonds. We all applauded, as did Swinging Beauty. Nothing became of George's love affair with Swinging Beauty as she moved from the village a short time later. Nevertheless, it was a day I will never forget.

Strange as it may seem, growing up in Ft. Jefferson seemed quite normal to me. Our neighbors were more than friends. They were more like family: a family that looked after one another, especially in times of trouble or sorrow. Maintaining contact with one another was a simple matter, especially in the summer when all doors and windows were open. In the winter, it was more of a challenge to be a part of everyone else's business, but Grandma Z had found a way. My mother's mother found the solution in the form of the new fangled telephone system. Grandma Z was a nanny of sorts and spent a great deal of her life raising the children of doctors from surrounding communities. She owned the house in which we lived and the building was loosely divided into grandma's side and our side. In the 1950's we still had a hand water pump in my grandmother's sink, a functional two-hole outhouse by the alley, a real toilet on "our side" and a wall hanging telephone. You knew if a phone call was for your house by the number of times the phone rang. You also knew when everyone else in town was called. Dad and Mom made it clear that listening in on other phone conversations was "verboten" and we followed the rules. Apparently, they never

explained these rules to Grandma Z or any of the other ladies of Fort Jefferson. I still remember the day, as a high school student, I was talking on the phone to a close friend. Upon finishing my conversation I said goodbye to my friend and finished by saying, "And, goodbye Gladys, goodbye Nellie, goodbye Loani, goodbye Alice and so one." Each goodbye was followed by a subtle click. Unfortunately, my mother overheard my fun and explained to me that it was rude and inappropriate behavior. I'm still not sure it was, but I honored Mom's wishes and never repeated the sin.

Chapter #3: Claude & Summy

On numerous occasions over the years my children have whined, "I'm bored." I would look to my left and see Nintendo. To my right I would see Sega. Behind me would stand the BIG SCREEN television and to the front two cats and a dog. I never understood their dilemma. My world as a child was somewhat different. To the right was Claude and Summy's general store. To my left was the five-mile hike to Uncle Dick's farm. Straight ahead was my one-mile escape route to Wayne Lakes Park and to the rear and down the hill was the "Thinking Tree." The Thinking Tree was the place where my two brothers and I always stopped when we were running away from home due to some social injustice Mom and Dad inflicted upon us. To this day, I cannot remember being bored, even if it meant spending a day chipping away at an anthill and watching the little red devils rebuild it.

Story #10: The Home of the Eagle

Claude and Summy were two very special people. It is almost impossible for me to say one name without the other. They were an inseparable pair. The untrained urban eye might think them a bit unpolished and uneducated. After surviving life in the coalmine country of West (By God) Virginia, Claude and Summy pulled up stakes and headed west to real civilization - Fort Jefferson, Ohio. Their general store was a lot like Mecca to my brother John and me. There was hardly a day go by, especially during summer vacation, that we didn't spend at least a few brief moments or a few long hours in that wonderful establishment. The sights, sounds and smells color my memories to this very day.

Claude was a raw-boned man. If he could have stood up straight, I would guess his height to have been about 6-foot, 3-inches. However, the coalmines put a permanent kink in his back that left him perpetually staring at the ground. He was soft spoken and his physical distortion hid his remarkable strength. Behind the store Claude yearly hand cultivated a two-acre garden that always produced an incredible bounty of green, yellow, orange, gold, brown, red and other multiple-colored stuff. It all tasted good. I know that because frequently I would sneak into the garden and pilfer a few goodies, especially the pears that hung from the tree located at the southeast corner. In fact, the only bad thing about Claude's magnificent garden was an English walnut tree. I'll explain my distain for this tree in a later story.

Summy was a sometimes-stern woman of significant size, but not fat, who had a heart of gold and a marvelous sense of wit and wry. An accident confined her to a wheelchair, but it never dampened her spirit. Watching Summy negotiate the store in her wheelchair was a lot like watching Mario Andretti negotiating a Grand Prix course. Summy also dipped snuff and that meant that spittoons had to be strategically staggered about the store. These came in handy for the local farmers who preferred chewing tobacco.

Evenings were a favorite time to visit Claude and Summy because the best television shows were on then. Besides the seven stick and metal chairs that surrounded the potbellied stove, Claude and Summy had two special stuffed chairs that looked directly at the TV. One was reserved for Claude and the other belonged to whoever could get there first. Summy remained in her wheelchair. When the television was clicked on, everyone would take a seat. As a child, I imaged that it was a lot like going to the opera, but I learned later in life that Claude and Summy's show was more memorable and a lot easier to understand. Occasionally I would look over to see if Claude had dozed off. Claude didn't talk much and sometimes I was uncertain about his consciousness. Then, as if by magic, Big Time Wrestling would appear on the screen.

Even as a young child, there was just something that didn't seem right about those wrestlers. My brothers and I fought – sometimes just for fun. However, here were great big men in strange, tight suits flying all over the place. Being the young cowboy that I was, it was only natural I knew that Don Eagle, the only wrestling Indian, was the only true wrestler of the bunch. For some reason Claude and Summy believed everything they watched was real, and Summy would really let them have it if they cheated, especially Dangerous Dan. Claude would normally nod in agreement, but never say a word.

DON EAGLE

During breaks in the action, it would not be unusual to see a shadow circling overhead. When I would look up, there it would be. It never failed. In addition, the sight of it would cause my body to freeze solid – as if a single movement might bring about some unforeseen, terrible event. It was the Eagle! No, not Don Eagle. Just, "The Eagle."

Around Fort Jefferson, this eagle had gained nearly mythological proportions. It would circle overhead for what seemed like hours, occasionally swooping down to a lower altitude and then zipping back up to its previous height and continuing to circle. Its movements were menacing as it undulated and swooped. With each swoop, my body would tense and flinch. I knew the eagle would eventually land, but where was always a great mystery. The eagle had strong talons that would lock onto the eagle's landing site with incredible force. Would it be a neck, a leg, maybe a shoulder? You just never knew and the expectations increased to a feverish level. Suddenly, just as you lost your concentration, the eagle would drop out of the sky - like a bullet - and clamp onto its target. It was the worst when the eagle targeted your thigh, just behind the knee, as this site caused you to writhe in the chair, frantically trying to release the eagle's grip.

It was impossible to release the bony, but extremely strong, fingers of Claude the Eagle, but if you could just hold out until the commercial was over, all would be well. Thank God, commercials were shorter in those days.

-30-

The ever-increasing population and urban sprawl along with the stay-at-home technology pacifiers and the public's irrational belief that everything can be made perfectly safe has muzzled many of the activities that were not only fun but also exciting and educational for the youth of Fort Jefferson. Grandma Z used to say that the Good Lord looks over the children, and I think she was right. Of course, she also said, "God gives pretty children to ugly people to make them feel better." Regardless, there were many times I am sure that only God's intervention kept my brothers and me from being killed – not to mention the risk we caused our neighbors. The Good Lord knows that my brothers and I never would have purposely hurt Claude or Summy, but one summer day we came close to giving a terrible thrill. And, that carries us along the thread to my next story.

Story #11: God, Don't Let Him Die

In our youth, my brothers John, Bob and I, who were each three years apart, were always known as the "Light Brothers." We were never singled out. Instead, we were thought of as one single organism. I was the youngest of the three and my very own mother, when wanting my immediate presence, would shout, "Johnbobbill." At school my teachers would say, "Oh, you're one of the Light Brothers." I kinda believed that I understood how the Wright Brothers felt at Kitty Hawk, but there were only two of them.

The Light Brothers

The Light Brothers were not destructive by nature. We had a zest for life and a zest for learning. It was Dad who usually got us started on some hobby or sport that usually eventually got us into trouble of some sort. Such was the case when Dad came home from work one day with a metal rocket he had constructed. This was not a cardboard rocket such as children use today. It was made of solid metal (about 5 inches in diameter, 3 feet high), and it used very special solid fuel. On launch day, Dad and the Light Brothers carried the rocket down near the Thinking Tree and positioned the launching pad in the middle of the county road. We had no sophisticated electronic launch system, only the dynamite fuse we got from Shorty Longfellow. We lit the long fuse, and then headed the 1/4-mile trek back up the hill to the house. There wasn't much traffic in those days, so we didn't have to worry much about a truck/rocket collision.

It was a sight to behold when the rocket fuel ignited and the missile streaked vertically, parting the air and going rapidly out of sight. We never found any trace of the rocket, but it made no difference – the Light Brothers were in the rocket business. Dad lost interest, but we brothers divided the design and build responsibilities, and started building rockets. My job was to engineer fuels. Bob sketched up the overall mechanical designs and John machined the parts. The Lighthouse had a full-fledged machine shop in its basement where the design and build operations took place.

Black powder was readily available, but it did not produce enough energy to satisfy the Light Brothers' thirst for power and altitude. It came to me one day (in a letter from Huntsville, Alabama, but that's another story) that black-powdered zinc and sulfur might make a great fuel. It did, but the proportional mix and distribution were critical to performance. Our first rockets were small aluminum shells using black powder for propulsion. When we switched to my new fuels, the intense heat melted the nozzles and the rocket bodies; therefore, stainless steel became the material of choice.

The above detail in rocket design might make you wonder what this has to do with Claude and Summy. Well, a strange chain of events brought about a near calamity that could have cost Claude his life, or perhaps worse.

As the mad chemist, I was in a state of constant design. Over time, I had perfected the perfect blend of my zinc/sulfur concoction, but on the day of perfection, I was able to make a very limited quantity of the fuel. Unfortunately, some of the less-than-quality fuels also remained on hand. On the very same day, Middle Brother John had just finished a nice new stainless steel rocket. As luck would have it, Elder Brother Bob brought home some of his high school classmates that day and wanted to impress them with a rocket launch.

Down to the basement we went to prepare the missile for service. As Bob poured my new fuel into the shining rocket body, there was only enough to fill the rocket about three-quarters full. Bob reached for an older lot of fuel to complete the fill.

"Don't use that!" I warned.

"Why not?" he sneered.

"It's not good. The output is low as is the burn rate. It's unstable," I cautioned.

"It'll be okay," he assured.

Bob was always very reassuring, but in this case, I was sure the consequences might not be the best.

"No kidding. It's not good," I pleaded.

Pleading never worked very well with Bob. He was a natural born leader. He even was an Eagle Scout, so to say he was self-assured was an understatement.

"Don't worry. It's okay," he said as he filled the remainder of the rocket body and attached the spun steel nozzle.

Well, shucks! Who really knew just how that rocket would perform? Besides, a lengthy argument with Bob in front of his friends was never a good idea. Bob was six years older – nearly an adult and eligible for 3/2 beer.

With our smaller rockets, we used a sloped launching rail to send the device skyward at a 62-degree angle. This not only reduced the initial required impulse of the engine to lift the bird, but also allowed us to launch from the road beside our yard. It also gave us a chance to recover the missiles down range in Shorty Longfellow's field. If we could not find them, Shorty always did when he plowed the fields in the spring. He always knew where to return them.

Let me refresh the picture. We have a rocket filled 3/4-full with a highly effective and explosive fuel. The remaining 1/4 space, the first to be ignited, is a less-than-perfect fuel. We have several untrained high school observers, two excited Light Brothers, one anxious Light Brother and, finally, someone who escaped our notice as we assembled the launching rail on the middle of the county road.

If you recall, Claude and Summy's store sat just across the county road to the north of our house, and Claude's precious garden sat directly north of our launching rail. It was a fine summer day, and Claude was hoeing his garden as usual. In addition, as usual, Claude's upper torso was bent parallel to the ground as he patiently chopped the weeds from each row. We didn't notice Claude. Don't judge us! Do you think NASA would notice some guy hoeing a garden across the road? I don't think so.

Bob carefully placed the rocket on the rail at the proper position. I ran the ignition wires to the site and attached them to the igniter in the nozzle. All was set for countdown. We all huddled behind our wooden blockhouse; the 10-second countdown commenced as John and I scanned for oncoming automobile traffic, which sometimes forced a temporary hold. 10-9-8-7-6-5-4-3-2-1-"Ignition" – "Liftof-f-f-f-f-f-f." But, the rocket sat stationary in the rail. Without warning a sputtering sound began emitting from the rocket's nozzle and smoke curled skyward. Then the rocket lurched ahead and plummeted off the end of the rail, falling the short distance to the absolute crown of the county road.

It's important to have an understanding about things like the "crown of the road." It is called the "crown" because it is the highest point of the roadway – a straight line at the highest point going down the center of the roadway. I make this point because the middle of the missile landed precisely in the middle of the crown, and the rocket was converted to a highly volatile teeter-totter. Its sputtering and unstable engine gave the missile just enough energy to tip up and down and spin around like a sadistic carnival ride. As unexpected as it began, the sputtering stopped and the rocket ceased its motion, balanced precariously in the middle of the road.

It was at this time that we first noticed Claude hoeing his garden. I'm not sure how my brothers felt, but I felt like a golf ball lodged in my throat. The rocket was aimed precisely at Claude's elevated butt as he slowly moved down a garden row that was perfectly aligned with the missile's apparent launch angle.

Bob immediately tried to make contact with God. I distinctly remember him saying, "Oh God!" It's strange how God becomes very real at times like this. I also remember asking," God, please don't let him die."

I have to tell you that I would have preferred not being the chemist who produced the fuel in those anxious moments. My lofty ideals regarding the wisdom of Eagle

Scouts also was shattered. Worst of all was my singular knowledge about the super fuel that was being approached by heat from the smoldering, failed fuel.

I would have given my life away in those few seconds to save Claude. Just at about the time I was getting my wits together, the new fuel ignited, and with a roar the missile headed directly for Claude's hinter side. My world stopped and space-time slowed to a snail's pace so I could watch every agonizing inch the rocket traveled. The entire event probably lasted less than one second.

God was watching and the rocket screamed no more than six non-exaggerated inches over Claude's vulnerable backside and it continued to gain altitude, finally leaving Fort Jefferson airspace to the north.

The older guys celebrated. I sat down. Claude simply rolled his head to the right and gazed skyward for a few seconds, and then continued hoeing his garden.

-30-

Now, you would think an event like our last story would scare young folks out of the rocket business, but you wouldn't be thinking clearly. Actually, the Light Brothers continued their missile program well into the future, primarily because no responsible adult saw us nearly shish kabob our beloved neighbor. We will talk more about the space program at Cape Fort Jefferson in later stories, but one more story about Claude and Summy is in order, but this story did not have a happy ending.

Story #12: Please Ask Your Dad

I moved away from Fort Jefferson for several years but maintained touch with family and friends and on rare visits I would stop over to say "howdy" to my second parents, Claude and Summy. As they aged it became harder and harder for them to deal with simple chores. It was not easy for Summy to move from her bed in the back of the store to her wheelchair. Sometimes she would slip to the floor and the combined strength of Summy and Claude could not return her body to bed or wheelchair. This had never been a problem when Brother John and I lived at home, because Claude would call and we would assist Claude in returning Summy to mobility. Now, the government had called John to Vietnam, and I was living in faraway Michigan.

It was a hard time for Summy and Claude's son and daughter-in-law, who lived in the next house north of the store. Town folks, with the best intentions, injected their opinions regarding what should be done with Claude and Summy.

"They can't take care of themselves anymore."

"How can you let them live like this?"

"It's a disgrace. You have to do something."

The pressure became too much and Claude and Summy were trucked to a nursing home, five miles north to the metropolis of Greenville.

I had not heard of the move to the nursing home in Greenville, so it came as a great shock when I returned home for a visit and saw the old store barren and dark, with gasoline pumps rusting and old signs flopping in the mild breeze.

At first I thought, "This is probably a good thing. A good nursing home together where meals are served on a regular basis and Summy can be helped in an out of bed is the best thing."

I worried more about Claude than Summy. Claude was in better health, but Summy was feisty and not prone to be kept down. Claude had always stayed in good physical shape by working his garden for hour after hour, from spring planting through summer cultivating to fall harvest. Summy had always kept in shape by manipulating her wheelchair throughout the store obstacle course.

The next day I decided to pay my extended parents a surprise visit. I drove to the nursing home, and upon entering through the double doors, I was greeted by a strong medicinal smell that had none of the old store's lived-in fragrances of spittoons and snuff. The walls were stark white and gave off a glare from the overhead florescent lighting. It didn't have the many, wonderful cardboard signs with ornery sayings plastered at odd angles on an entire wall. Nor did it have a stately potbellied stove or a giant, hand-cranked cash register that you could open and close, just for fun, and listen to the bells.

I walked to the counter and asked if it might be okay to visit with Claude and Summy. A very rigid-looking woman with a tight-fitting, gray suit asked, "Whom do you wish to visit first?"

"What?" I asked.

"I said, 'whom do you wish to visit first?'" she said tersely.

My mind could not comprehend what she was asking. Why would I want to visit one or the other first?

"I want to visit both of them," I confusedly continued.

"You said that already. Do you want to visit Mr. or Mrs. Shaffer?" she complained.

In my entire life, I had never thought of Claude and Summy as two separate entities. They were not. They were one, single, solitary force that had affected my life from the day I was born. To think that anyone would separate such a powerful force was beyond my comprehension.

The woman scribbled down two room numbers and directed me down the hallway. When the first number appeared, I walked in. It was a small room with two beds and in the first bed was Summy. She looked gaunt and haggard. In the second bed was another woman who was groaning and moaning in a continuous cadence. It took several minutes for Summy to recognize me, but she did, and we talked for some time. Her speech was hesitant and her normal confidence and spirit was gone. She talked of Claude as if he lived a million miles away and she wondered how he was doing. It was a sad visit for me, but conversation with Summy in no way prepared me for my next visit.

Summy fell asleep during our conversation, and I chose to take the opportunity to travel down the sterile corridor to see Claude. When I entered the room, I was not surprised to find Claude in another two-bed, closet-sized room with a male roommate.

Claude resembled people I had seen in films showing holocaust victims. He was sitting in a chair beside his bed, his upper torso leaning forward and his chin nestled between his palms. Claude recognized me immediately. Before we had time to engage in conversation, a nurse came to the room and removed Claude's roommate from the premises. What followed next left a dark mark in the depths of my soul that remains to this very day.

Claude looked me square in the eyes and, while tears trickled down his cheeks, very firmly said, "Bill, tell your Dad he has got to bring me a gun here. Please, tell him to bring me a gun. You've gotta tell him. Please, get me a gun."

I didn't have to ask why he wanted a gun. There was no more conversation as Claude placed his head back between his hands and rocked side to side.

"How could people be so cruel?" I wondered. What had been done to Claude and Summy was akin to a frontal lobotomy, where a single human brain is split into two pieces in the name of science. I left the building in tears and it turned out to be the last time I saw Claude and Summy, both of whom died, in separate rooms, a short time later.

-30-

Human beings, in the name of kindness, can be very cruel. Science has yet to find a way to quantify a single entity like Claude and Summy. As self-centered feminists, abusive husbands and other anti-family movements destroy the very fabric of the homes in America, it is unlikely that science will have enough samples on the subject to learn how two human beings can actually be one. Claude and Summy didn't understand such things as relational dominance as they were a single unit. It has been hard for me to forgive those who divided this singularity, despite their good intention.

When I married and started a family of my own, I learned just how difficult it is to be at one with one's spouse. Personality clashes, societal expectations, lack of trust brought on by misinterpretation of verbal or body language, and differences in needs for the "things" of life are all forces that do their best to keep couples apart.

I never learned to master the art shown to me by Claude and Summy, but I am very thankful that God gave me such an example of bonding, because this knowledge always gave me hope that such love is possible, even if it comes in a future life.

Chapter #4: Cape Fort Jefferson

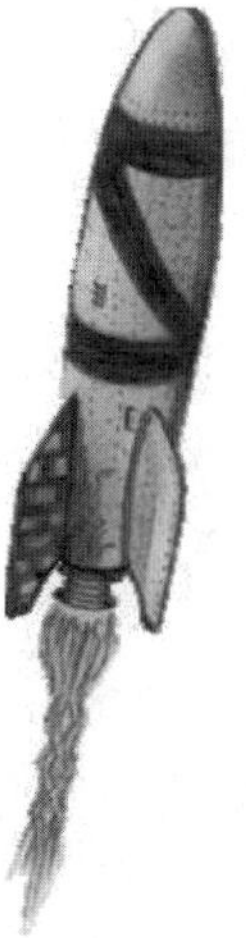

One must put things in context when listening to stories. The 1950's and 1960's were eventful years in American history, and Fort Jefferson was not immune. We had just finished World War II, and the future was looking bright as America captured German high technology and began to rebuild the world with its hyperactive industrial base. Dad already had launched us in the space race when he brought the large metal rocket home and showed us its exciting power. We were of Swiss and German heritage from several sides of the family, so we tended to put the best face on the war and looked for the good in the German people. We abhorred their leadership. I loved their rockets.

Story #13: My Heroes

At various stages in my life, I was told that I was not a normal child. It has never seemed like fair criticism. At the age of 12, my heroes were probably the same as most of my peers. Don Eagle, Roy Rogers, The Lone Ranger, Commando Cody and Superman were a few of the top contenders. However, at age 13, my interests shifted to a different plane, and so did my heroes.

For some reason I had developed a strong interest in inertial guidance systems. This electro-mechanical magic kept rockets on course as they traversed the heavens. There was no Internet in those days, and many libraries had deliberately banned technical papers from Germany, so finding information about such things was difficult at best, especially in Ft. Jefferson.

Dad

One day I explained my frustration to Dad. He explained that the best knowledge in the United States resided in the minds of the captured German scientists who had developed the German rocket program. He also explained that, in his opinion, these scientists just wanted to build rockets and that they were not particularly interested in wars.

I asked Dad where they were. He said that our government had locked them up at White Sands, New Mexico, immediately following the war, but that he had heard they recently moved to a place called Huntsville, Alabama, near the Redstone Arsenal. Dad pointed out that the top dog of knowledge in inertial guidance systems was a guy named Wernher von Braun.

I went to my room and authored a brief letter to this hotshot scientist named Wernher von Braun. The letter explained my strong curiosity about inertial guidance systems and my frustration about not being able to learn about such things in Fort Jefferson, Ohio. I had no address and no way to find one, so I simply addressed it to:

Wernher von Braun
General Delivery
Huntsville, Alabama

Then, I dropped the letter in the mailbox in front of the house, where I knew Dutch would faithfully pick it up in the morning. That was that.

Now most people would not expect an answer if they sent a personal letter to the president of the United States. My parents probably felt that way about my possibilities of ever hearing from such a celebrity as Wernher von Braun. But, I expected him to answer. I had no reason to think otherwise. Wernher had never let me down before. Why would he do so on my very first letter? Logic at the age of 13 can be a bit convoluted.

Only two weeks had elapsed when a rather large envelope arrived at the Lighthouse, and it was addressed to "William Light," and the return address was "Huntsville, Alabama." I tore the envelope open and there it was: a three page, hand-written letter from the spaceman himself – Dr. Wernher von Braun. Von Braun went into great *detail about the principals of inertial guidance and he even sketched out the principals on a level that I clearly understood.*

In the year and one-half of corresponding with Dr. von Braun, I learned of his colleagues like Willey Ley and Walter Dornberger. I learned how liquid fuel rockets circulated the cool fuels and oxidizers through tubing around the engine nozzles to keep the engine from melting due to the intense heat. Moreover, he taught me about solid fuel propellants and he thought that I might wish to experiment with mixtures like black powdered zinc and sulfur, as he did as a child. I took Dr. von Braun's advice regarding black powdered zinc and sulfur and learned the scientific methods needed to study and manufacture the proper mixtures. My fuels helped to successfully power many of the Light Brothers' missiles that frequently launched from Cape Fort Jefferson.

-30-

Of course, my greatest hero was my father, who seemed to be a man who could do anything. Dad always taught by example, and I never was forced to learn. Learning around the Lighthouse was a very natural and enjoyable thing. So was doing. Sometimes the Light Brothers tended to do a little too much as is illustrated in our next story.

Story #14: John's Whistling Nose Cone

My Brother John was a mechanic. I'm convinced that he was born that way. Mom never said anything about him coming into the world with a screwdriver in one hand and pliers in the other, but I'll bet he did.

Even as a young man of 16, John could conceive of and build things that were well beyond his years. In our basement machine shop, he was a lathe hand and could operate just about any machine imaginable. He also was a skilled artisan with hand tools and he knew how to create imaginative machining processes. It was only natural that John would do most of the metalwork during our expanding missile production.

During our rocket-building evolution, one persistent problem nagged us. Our rockets were high performance, even by today's standards. Consequently, by using the 62-degree launching angle, our rockets would roar into the great beyond and disappear forever unless Shorty would happen to find them during spring plowing.

John came up with an exciting, potential solution.

"I got thinking about this last night," John excitedly reported. "I think I can design a nose cone for one of our rockets that will whistle. We can use compressed air at high velocity to check the effectiveness of the whistle," he explained.

"What good is a whistling rocket gonna do?" I asked.

"Well, I thought we could get the guys around town (we sometimes called Fort Jefferson a town) and give them each a flag and then space them out downrange," John continued. "Then if they hear the rocket go overhead, they can wave the flag. If the rocket passes on their right side, they can wave to the right. If it passes left, wave left. What do ya think?"

It sounded like a good idea to me, so we started manufacturing white flags using pieces of white shirts found in the old clothes barrel and bamboo rods scavenged from a discarded window blind.

The rocket upon which the high-tech nose cone would be mounted was about four feet long and weighed about 18 pounds fully loaded. Since we needed a long visual path, we elected not to launch from the county road. Instead, we set up our launch rail in the side ditch behind the garage, using one of Shorty Longfellow's fence posts as a convenient support.

It was a hot and dry summer afternoon when we assembled our 12-member ground crew of excited flag wavers. We carefully distributed them, equidistantly spaced about 200 yards apart. We attached the ignition wires and prepared to launch. Our countdowns by this time were routine and the launch went off without a hitch. The rocket streaked into the air with a resounding swoosh, and in less than two seconds, we could hear the shrieking nose cone.

In a few more seconds, the rocket was approaching our down range observers, and they waved frantically as it passed over their heads. Our last observer was approximately 3/4-mile down range, and when he waved his flag, we knew we had underestimated the rocket's range.

We also had underestimated the dryness of the long grass in the side ditch. By the time we noticed, nearly 50 yards of ditch was engulfed in flames, heading both east and south away from Shorty Longfellow's corner post, which also was in flames.

Before long, it seemed as if half of Fort Jefferson was attacking the inferno with everything from wet brooms to buckets of water and sand. It took about one hour to get things back into control, and since Mom had been manning a wet broom, we figured that things might be a bit quiet around the supper table that night. They were!

When Dad arrived home from work and saw the carnage created by our wonderful missile, he cut off all funding of our rocket program and nixed all future construction and launches. His attitude reminded me a lot of the Federal Government, so we had no choice but to take our operations underground.......but that's another story.

-30-

It wasn't as if we were trying to burn the town to the ground. Even Wernher von Braun had a few A4's (V2's) blow up on the launching pad during development. Moreover, the U.S. Navy didn't do any better with its Vanguard program. If it had not been for Dr. von Braun and the Redstone rocket with its modified V2 architecture, we would have been years behind those Russians and that darned Sputnik.

Underground the Light Brothers went.

Story #15: Two Stages of Glory

It's one thing to make a single stage, solid fuel rocket. It's quite another to create a high performance two or three stage missile. And, it's even more of a challenge to keep all of your rocket research and manufacturing in total secret, especially when your operation is situated directly under the main living area of your parents' home.

I've heard lots of seemingly honest folks tell about how, when they were kids, they were totally open with their parents. They say they told their parents every intimate detail of their lives. I have to be honest here, 'cause I promised I would. We held many things back from our parents. Not out of meanness. We just didn't want to scare them to death.

John's whistling nose cone was a great success. Wernher von Braun didn't quit when the U.S. government locked him away in a desert camp, so why should we give up just because of a little fire. Well, maybe it wasn't so little, but golly whiz, our work was important.

So underground, quite literally, we went. Our rock-walled basement wasn't the most comfortable workspace I've ever seen. It was inhabited by numerous critters like spiders and an occasional mouse. The oil furnace resided there, and it was reasonably warm during the winter months. We became kind of a "Hole in the Ground Gang." Considering my love of cowboys in my youth, it made some sense, but now that I was all grown up at 13, it was time to get down to the business of building "real" rockets. We were about to do Wernher proud.

Security was always at risk. Mom occasionally told neighbors, friends and even total strangers, "They are good boys." Mom always thought children had a sort of innocence that protected them from doing "naughty" things. I always hated the word "naughty." I thought perhaps it be a naval word meaning something like, "a small, tipsy, sailing vessel that nobody should be caught dead in." Anyway, Mom most likely would not recognize the hardware and fuels we were using in our clandestine operation. So, scratch her off as a big risk. Now Dad - that was a very different matter.

My father, who seemed to know a lot about everything and could throw a masking-tape covered 3/4" washer in the air and shoot a hole through its middle with a 22-caliber rifle, was our biggest worry. For one thing, he was the guy who issued the edict and, at least in words, closed our operations. What was a child to do?

I think that the security measures we took guarding our top-secret project helped me later in life. For example, my teenage daughter tried to experiment with cigarette smoking. She sneaked out of her bedroom window in the dead of winter to my small camper trailer that was parked in the yard behind our house. With my childhood experience about subterfuge, it didn't take me long to solve the crime. Of course, it helped that there was two feet of snow on the ground when she snuck out of her bedroom window and left a perfect set of footprints all the way to the trailer and back.

Our goal was simple – Build a two-stage, solid propellant rocket that would travel for many miles. It was a daunting task. The first stage had to have enough energy to lift itself and the second stage off the ground with enough instantaneous speed to keep it stable in flight. We had no gyroscopes, so we had to rely on air pressure and proper balance to keep our craft on course. The most challenging problems were how to ignite the second stage at the appropriate time and then jettison the first stage. This was a truly "explosive" problem. To discover the solutions required extensive test bench burns and these burns not only caused smoke but also noxious fumes. This meant that testing had to be postponed to the fall of the year. In Fort Jefferson, there was an annual ritual, "The Burning of the Leaves." When the fall colors fell to the ground, it was everyone's civic duty to burn leaves, days at a time. Leaves make lots of smoke and fragrance. The perfect cover for our testing that was carried out in our no-car garage. I almost hate to divulge this secret, as I know my mother will first learn about it while reading this book. However, it worked wonderfully, and by early winter, we had the kinks worked out of the design.

The winter months saw construction of our masterpiece get underway. Work went slowly as school sapped our time and energy. It didn't help that we always had to put the work pieces in various drawers and shelves, away from prying eyes. By spring, we had the routine down to a science. The characteristics of the old house worked like an early warning system. When anyone walked across the floor above our heads, their footsteps could be tracked with uncanny precision. If the kitchen door that led to the outside basement entryway was opened, it made a predictable squeaking noise that betrayed all who passed through it. Overhead footsteps always raised the tension in the shop and the door squeak meant instant cover-up of all work.

Our five-foot high work of genius had a five-inch diameter first stage and a three-inch diameter second stage. Based on burn rate, thrust, mass and planned-trajectory calculations we estimated that its potential range was four miles. Those who are technically astute will understand that this rocket was not your usual toy.

By early summer, we were ready for launch. However, when and how had to be carefully planned. Hindsight being 20/20, I can tell you that in our excitement to let the "bird" fly, our planning took a second seat to the "Zoweee" syndrome. Only by watching the movie "Mr. Roberts" will you understand the "Zoweee" syndrome. If you haven't seen Jack Lemon as Ensign Pulver in this movie, go rent it. Seeing his fulminate of mercury triumph in the ship's laundry room is the only way you'll understand the Light Brothers' emotions that fateful night. Go rent the movie!

It had to be a night launch so that the rocket's engine could glow as a bright beacon for in-flight tracking. It would be our first night launch. The air had to be still to reduce the possibility of trajectory alignment issues. With a four-mile range, low clouds were not acceptable. Moreover, all three of the Light Brothers had to be home at the same time.

Finally, the perfect night appeared, and we were ready. We randomly left the house in order not to draw undue attention from Mom and Dad. The rocket had been assembled for weeks. All that remained was to:

(1) Load the secret black-powdered zinc and sulfur fuel.
(2) Install the timed burn-through delay fuse into the junction tube between the two stages.
(3) Assemble the launch rail and set the appropriate angle.
(4) Pull the makeshift wooden "blockhouse" from the garage.
(5) Attach the ignition wires to the first stage igniter.
(6) Assemble the stages.
(7) Mount the rocket on the launch rail.
(8) Crouch behind the wooden "blockhouse."
(9) Start the countdown.
(10) Push the button

Now if it looks to you that we really had our act together, you would be thinking the same as the Light Brothers were that eventful and wondrous night. Unfortunately, we had overlooked two major things:

(1) No sound testing had been done with mock up engines, and the first stage engine was by far the largest motor we had ever made.

(2) No tests were run to determine how well sound traveled on a warm, still, muggy night in downtown Fort Jefferson.

We followed our checklists to the letter, and my heart felt like it was climbing into my throat. Then the familiar 10-second countdown began. It had been one whole year since we last heard it. 10-9-8-7-6-5-4-3-2-1----Liftoff. Unlike the rocket that nearly killed Claude Shaffer and lifted off with only a swoosh, our crowning glory leapt from the launch pad with a deafening roar. If I could write a word that defined the sound, I would, but I can't. Our hands, in unison, instinctively covered our ears, and we all slowly rose from behind our protective shield and gazed in awe as the bright white ball of fire blazed through the pitch black, moonless night sky.

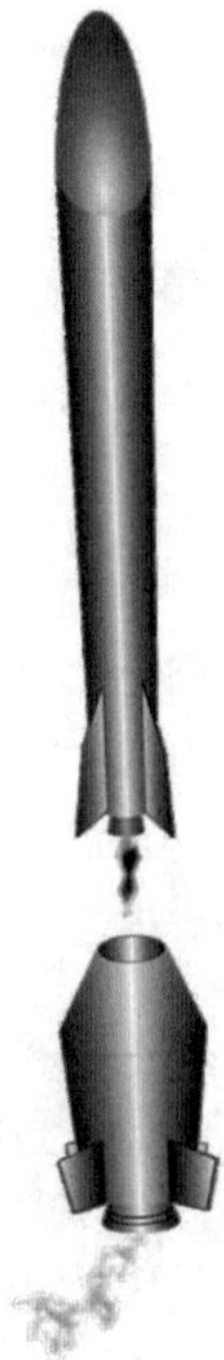

The rocket left Ft. Jefferson airspace in milliseconds and rapidly climbed altitude. As it was passing over Merl and Millie Fishback's farm, located about one-half mile down the county road past the Thinking Tree and just north of the S-curves, the ball of light suddenly extinguished. I'm not sure if my brothers prayed, but I did. "Come on…Come on baby....come on," I pleaded. My brothers were counting seconds aloud. Then it happened. Right on schedule another brilliant light appeared in the eastern sky. We all began counting the seconds. One .... Two .... Three ..... Four .... Five .... Six .... Seven ..... Eight ... KA-BOOOOOOM!!!!" it echoed through the town. It took eight seconds for the sound of the second stage ignition to reach us. "Great Scott!" I thought. Our greatest achievement was over one and one-half miles away and still accelerating. We continued to be mesmerized as the missile disappeared into darkness.

My mind started fantasizing about Wernher von Braun and how he must have felt as he watched his first rockets soar into the air. It was at this time that a looming figure appeared behind my brothers. Two large hands landed, one each, on my brothers' shoulders.

"What in the hell is going on out here?" Dad said, in a not-so-subdued voice.

We all stood in silence.

"Get that stuff off the road," he grumbled.

We all hustled to remove the launching rail and wires from the roadway. It had been a glorious night.

-30-

Dad never spoke another word as he turned to walk away. I was in better position to see Dad's face as he left, and I noticed something very unusual. He was smiling. It was an odd sort of smile. The kind you get when you're proud about something. I'll never know for sure, but I think he was proud of us in an odd sort of way. He did his fatherly duties, but all and all, I'm reasonably sure he was proud. I do know that he never asked us <u>not</u> to build rockets again.

How people think and learn has always been of interest to me. What causes a mind to absorb data, convert it into information, and then formulate knowledge from the patterns and shapes revealed in the information is a very powerful mystery. The ancient Egyptians had few technologies, but they did have tremendous organizational skills. Today's world is driven by technology, but organizational skills are waning. There was no doubt about that Dad's original silver rocket was the spark that kindled the technology fires in the Light Brothers' imaginations regarding rockets.

It is a sad testament to humanity, but throughout all history, it has been the wars that have given humankind its largest technological leaps. Even some of Wernher von Braun's huge successes came under wartime conditions at Peenemunde where slave labor was forced to build rockets under horrific conditions. No one will ever know for sure exactly how Werner von Braun felt about the war and the slave labor. My only direct knowledge came from how he treated a 13-year-old boy in a small Ohio village, and he treated him well and filled his mind with knowledge and expectations.

War is a curious thing. I fight against being judgmental. It has always been difficult for me to understand how politicians like the supposed savior of America, Franklin D. Roosevelt, who deliberately set out to provoke Japan to war and then allowed his fellow citizens to be sacrificed at Pearl Harbor in order to go to war in Europe and save the American economy, could make the decision he did. Those decisions reached their goals, but at what cost?

My best guess is that many politicians, like Roosevelt, studied an ancient Greek poem known as "The Barbarians on the Border."

Story #16: Barbarians on the Border (fiction?)

Once upon an ancient time there was a small Greek town that suffered terrible economic conditions and all of its people walked through the streets with their heads facing to the ground, their shoulders slumped forward, and they cried, "Woe are we. There is no food in the warehouses, our factories are not running, we have no crops in the fields, our soldiers have resigned, our children are starving, our shops are closed, our protective ramparts are decaying. What are we going to do? What are we going to do?"

Suddenly, a chariot with driver approached the town at breakneck speed, and as it passed over the village's cobblestone streets, the panicked driver excitedly shouted, "There are barbarians on the borders. There are barbarians on the border."

The townspeople looked up in disbelief and began making plans for the siege of the town that was sure to begin when the barbarians arrived. Work crews immediately began rebuilding the protective ramparts, in order to hold the barbarians out. The factories began manufacturing bows and arrows, slings, spears and shields for the warriors to use in the battles to come. To protect against the coming attack, the farmers tilled and planted the fields in order to fill the grain bins. Within two months, activities had risen to a feverish pitch. Everyone was working toward the common cause. Suddenly, another chariot with rider appeared in the distance. As it rattled over the village's cobblestone streets, the rider shouted, "There are no barbarians on the border.

There are no barbarians on the border." Without hesitation the townspeople looked toward the ground, their shoulders slumped forward, and they began crying, "What are we going to do? What are we going to do? What are we going to do?"

-30-

Such a story, such a mystery, and such wonderful insight from the ancient Greek poet. The barbarians never were on the border so, in reality, there was never a threat. Yet, the townspeople went from absolute poverty and destitution to a thriving community then dove back into despair, with no real change in surrounding conditions. Oh, how well politicians and dictators have learned this poem.

Fort Jefferson had its fair share of wars as I was growing up there. I have never been sure what caused these wars. They just seemed to happen. Technology never was at the cause, but in one war, it was technology that caused an enemy to flee. I mentioned in an earlier story that Claude and Summy had an English walnut tree next to their garden that I didn't like. It was not because it was English although the German side of my family never had many good things to say about the English. I know that the bad feelings went back a few years as one family ancestor in 1836 named his son William Wallace Light after the Scotsman that rebelled against English rule and started a revolution. Anyway, it has crossed my mind that the "Great Walnut Wars" may have been some of the inspiration that served as the precursor to the development of our rocket program.

Story #17: The Great Walnut Wars

Prior to their meteoric rise to success in rocketry, the Light Brothers were charged with a great responsibility. I've never understood who charged us with this great burden. I only know that by the time I was six years of age, I was recruited by my two older brothers to serve as a soldier on, quite literally, the home front.

Children in small villages seem to congeal into segregated globs of humanity during the winter months. For some unknown reason, during the summer, the isolated globs begin to reform into armed camps. In very small villages like Fort Jefferson, there are only enough kids to form two armed camps. Such was the case in 1952 when the youthful factions of our small town engaged in gorilla warfare.

As I've told you before, I always wanted to be a cowboy, so I had no idea what war was all about. I understood things like fighting Indians, chewing tobacco and roping steers, but I had to trust the judgment of my older brothers regarding armed confrontation with masses of enemies in close proximity.

Unbelievably, there were rules to the battles during these wars. They were not easy to remember. Apples, pears, tomatoes, water balloons were legal weapons, while rocks and walnuts were not. I was never sure about the objective in the various skirmishes because ground was taken and given up during the battles, but at day's end all land holdings ended up precisely as they had started.

Honestly, I cannot tell you which armed camp first broke the rules that summer. It could have been the Talrins-Klepper-Younce clan, or it might have been the Light-Cooper-Jones crew. All I know is that someone threw the first walnut, and all hell broke loose. Our backyard contained two black walnut trees, so our ammunition supply was good. The only other walnut tree in Fort Jefferson sat directly across the county road at the edge of Claude and Summy's garden and that tree was English. The tree was very prolific, like all of Claude's crops, and its walnuts were much larger than ours were. The battles continued day after day with no end in sight.

English Walnut

Escalation was one thing, but a double-dare breach of rules inspired one of the first Light Brother's technological leaps. A skirmish broke out between the opposing camps one hot and sticky summer afternoon and it blossomed into all-out walnut mania. The green grenades cascaded from one side of the county road to the other. My training had been sparse and my ducking skills had not been perfected. Consequently, I was taking hits in unusual numbers. When I made a break for the house, the ultimate war crime was committed. Someone in the opposing camp let go a rock that sailed across the road and struck the back of my head, knocking me to the ground in a stupor and opening a two-inch gap in my scalp that bled profusely. The blood and carnage struck fear in our enemy's hearts, and they fled the battleground.

This event caused my eldest Brother Bob to look towards technology for answers. Bob was 12 and wise in the ways of the world. He already was in scouting, and he was working towards his ultimate goal, the Eagle Scout merit badge. Unlike our adversaries, Bob was determined to play by the rules (Scouts did in those days). Bob deducted that we could strike fear into the hearts of our enemies and end the war for the last time.

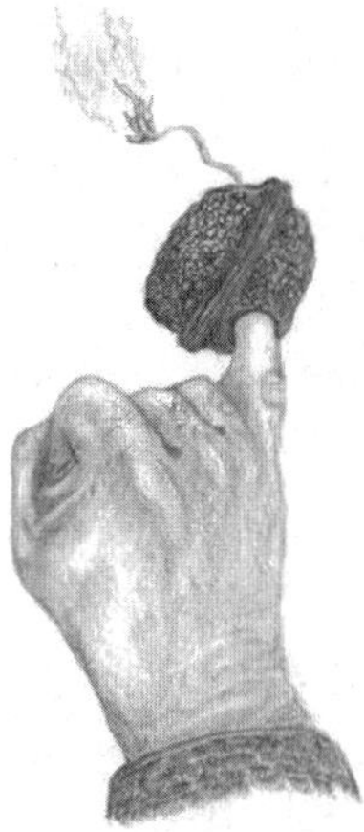

It did not take Bob long to find the answer. It came in the form of a large, dried walnut that had a cylindrical indentation on one side that just fit over the end of Bob's pinky finger, and a hollow center where worms had dissolved the kernel. Bob figured he could fill the hollow core with black gunpowder, attach a fuse and then launch the weapon high over the enemy's head where it would explode with a large white cloud of smoke and scare barbarians out of their wits.

Bob was very detailed and knew that wrapping his hand around such a grenade would not be safe in case of a premature ignition. That is where the pinky-finger-sized depression came in. He figured that he would stick the bomb on the end of his finger, have Brother John light the fuse, and then Bob would wing it with all of his might. It sounded good to me – but I didn't have to hold the bomb.

The day following the rock incident, we prepared in our basement work area for battle. The highly sophisticated walnut weapon was charged and fused. To the battleground we marched, set up our stations and waited for the enemy to appear. And, appear they did in full force. The battle was joined and walnuts began flying in profuse numbers from camp to camp. When it came time to unveil the secret weapon, John crawled to Bob's station. In the excitement, Bob jammed the walnut onto his pinky finger and lowered it to a position where John could light the fuse. The gray thread sputtered to life and Bob swung his arm with all the speed he could muster.

It's a shame I couldn't capture on movie film what happened next. Laurel and Hardy could not have done better. Bob's hurried loading of the bomb onto his pinky finger had caused the device to Lock onto his digit like a gator on a flamingo. Two more frantic swings failed to dislodge the grenade. Bob's eyes grew about two inches in diameter. In total desperation, he stretched his right arm skyward as far as it could possibly stretch, took his left hand and placed it over his left ear and waited for the inevitable explosion. And, explode it did, peeling the skin of Bob's pinky-turned-black-and-red finger like a monkey skinning a banana. The explosive poof and smoke and total spectacle did cause the enemy to flee, and Bob's goal of ending the walnut wars was achieved. We explained the hows, whys and wherefores about our secret weapon to our former enemies for many weeks thereafter. Moreover, we all learned much about black powder, wars, peace, fuses, and most of all, wedges.

When one reads a story, it is easy to miss the fine details. When one watches a story, the details make a lasting impression on the mind. My guess is that you missed the best part of the story because your imagination was not "watching." It occurred right before the bomb explodes. Go ahead. Go back and read it again. I will wait.

Did ya figure it out yet? No? Try again by forming a mental image of precisely how Brother Bob protected his hearing. Go on. You can do it. I will wait.

In the slight chance that your imagination failed you, here is the answer. Bob first stuck his right, bomb-laden arm straight up in the air, and then he placed his free left hand over his left ear that pointed safely at the ground. His unguarded right ear received the full force of the blast. You do strange things when under extreme duress.

Chapter #5: Special Moments

Stories often seem to transcend time and space. Fort Jefferson's brief continuum has been pocketed by many poignant stories. The following special moments highlight the diversity, individualism and spirit of some of those delightful beings that have never been clearly illuminated by the world spotlight.

Story #18: Polly Doesn't Want a Senator

James Milton Light was the father of James Wilbur Light who just happened to be my father. The senior Light had owned newspapers for most of his life, and he considered himself a "conservationist" - not to be confused with a "conservative." In his latter years, Granddad Light became the postmaster of the metropolis of Greenville, Ohio, and at one point he approached Fred Coppock, the CEO of American Aggregates Corporation, with the idea of reclaiming one of Fred's extensive gravel pits, and turning it into a lake-filled park and fish hatchery.

Granddad Light was an avid angler, and he authored a weekly outdoors column for the Greenville Daily Advocate until his death. Granddad was a Mason, and he was the founder of the Greenville Chapter of the National Association of Amalgamated Liars. You see, granddad figured any fisherman, by natural evolution, had to be a liar; therefore, it was only fitting to have an organization that did anglers justice.

This fun-loving elder Light happened to be the recipient of a special inheritance from an elder cousin who preceded him in death. The gift was Polly, a full-sized red and green South American parrot that was at the ripe old age of 70 years at the time of the inheritance.

Polly was no ordinary parrot. Polly could sing all the verses to the "old Rugged Cross" hymn without hesitation. Polly's command of the English language was profound and most of the Light family came to understand that Polly could reason quite well.

Granddad Light was well versed in the unpredictability of parrots since he had witnessed a remarkable happening in his former home in South Charleston, Ohio. This event occurred at the Christmas Eve service of the local Methodist church. The minister's wife had purchased a parrot and taught it to yell out "Praise the Lord." She talked her husband into allowing the parrot and cage to be set in front of the sermon pulpit for the service, believing that the occasional "praise-the-Lord" squawk would be inspirational. However, since Methodist churches have two pulpits in their sanctuaries, the minister's artistic wife felt the singular parrot made things appear unbalanced. She returned to the pet shop where she learned another parrot and cage, exactly like hers, recently sold to a local man. She asked if she could borrow the spare parrot for the Christmas Eve service, and the request graciously was granted.

Can you imagine the beauty of the situation? Here were two Christmas red-and-green parrots in identical cages gracing the two Methodist pulpits. The service began without incident. Finally, the time came when the minister entered the sermon pulpit and began his Yuletide lesson. The serene scene resembled a Norman Rockwell painting. A mouse could have been heard scurrying across the floor, when, suddenly, the silence was broken with the minister in mid-sentence. The sermon-pulpit

parrot chortled, "Praise the Lord!" Within milliseconds, the borrowed parrot chimed in with a hellish voice shouting, "Go to hell!" Pulpit parrot answered the challenge with another shriek, "Praise the Lord!" The satanic parrot screamed, "Go to hell!" The horrific teeter-totter verbal battle continued without abatement until anxious parishioners hurriedly dragged the two parrots out of the sanctuary.

Yes, Granddad Light was wise in the way of parrots; however, he was especially proud of Polly, and he routinely bragged about Polly's vocal gifts. He was especially fond of watching Polly imitate grandma Light's voice. Polly would sit in her kitchen cage and call, "Here kitty, kitty kitty." When the family cat would dash into the kitchen expecting a treat from Grandma Light, Polly would break into laughter, "ha, ha, ha, ha, haaaah!"

Senator Atwood visited Granddad Light one Sunday afternoon. The senator was excited about meeting Polly since he had heard so many stories about the oral genius. When Granddad and the senator approached the cage, Polly's head tilted to and fro with one eye firmly affixed on the senator. With no warning, Polly pivoted on her perch and clearly announced, "I won't talk!" And, he didn't for the rest of the day.

-30-

Some people believe that animals cannot think, but there is no question in my mind that Polly not only could think but also had a great sense of humor. After granddad Light's death, my Uncle Dick, the veterinarian, adopted Polly. Dick and wife, Lillian, had a beautiful daughter named Mary Arline who died of cancer at a very young age. Polly loved Mary Arline and relished mimicking her voice. When Mary Arline passed on, circumstances forced Uncle Dick into giving Polly a new home when Polly could not quit crying in Mary Arline's voice.

Story #19: Loani and Ann

After my father, a lifetime smoker, died of lung cancer, my mother moved to the "big city," Greenville, and my Brother John and his bride Ann moved into the old homestead. Ann adapted quickly to life in Fort Jefferson and soon made many friends. One of these friends was Loani.

Loani was in advanced years, small in stature and as wiry as a bristle brush. I had learned many of my first "dirty" stories from Loani prior to leaving Fort Jefferson at age 18. Ann, who was raised in a large 12-child Catholic family, quickly earned Loani's respect, and soon the pair groomed a warm and lasting friendship. It was one of those special relationships that few people achieve in their lifetimes; a bonding that transcends space and time.

Loani had experienced hard and sad times in her life, but her resilient spirit kept her high on life. She lost her husband and one son early in their respective lives. Loani had never been able to resolve her intellectual conflict concerning a loving and all-powerful supreme being, and the sudden deaths of her spouse and child. Grandma Z used to say, "The Lord works in mysterious ways," and I personally think that God was responsible for drawing Loani and Ann together. Ann, a devout Catholic, had married my brother, a faithful Methodist turned Presbyterian, and she most likely was trying to understand this mysterious God herself.

Ann and Loani would spend time together just talking, reading, doing a few crafts or perhaps telling stories, sometimes dirty ones I'm sure. Her eyesight was not perfect and she was forced to wear thick glasses. I remember the time when I returned home from Michigan to visit friends and family and I stopped in to see how Loani was doing. During the visit, I asked Loani, a voracious reader, "Are you still reading as much as you used to?"

Loani pulled the coke-bottle-lens glasses from her stubby nose, gazed across the room and stated, "No! It hurts my nose too much."

I can imagine that holding a book, sliding it back and forth across your nose and reading a one line at a time, could be a bit painful.

During one of Ann's visits with the proud and wise old woman, Loani confided to Ann about the anger she felt concerning God and his premature taking of the lives of her husband and son. She told Ann, "You'll know when I meet God, he's got some powerful explaining to do to me, and I plan on getting some answers."

A short time later Loani passed from this earth, and a funeral was set to be held in the cemetery on the hill, located about 300 yards south of the village. It was a beautiful cemetery. It was surrounded by farm fields. Its long entry road led from the state highway that passed north-and-south through the village. It was well maintained and its old hardwood, spruce and pine trees towered over our ancestors with a great dignity and grace.

Most of Loani's friends and family had preceded her in death. So on the day of the funeral, those who paid their respects included the minister, a few funeral home helpers and Ann. It was a beautiful day. There was not a single cloud in the sky, the sun shined brightly through the trees, and a gentle breeze caressed Ann's golden hair. It was a sad day for Ann, and her mind was stirring the pages of the many stories she and Loani had either passed on to one another or created themselves.

All was quiet as the minister began to speak a few words over Loani's suspended casket. Suddenly, without any warning, there came a vivid flash of light and the crashing sound of thunder that startled the sparse gathering of mourners and struck the pastor dumb. All present stood in stunned silence, except Ann who first smiled and then burst into uncontrollable laughter. You see, as Loani had predicted, Ann knew that Loani had just met God, and she knew that God had a lot of explaining to do.

-30-

Grandma Z was right. The Lord does work in mysterious ways. Grandma Z and my mother both sported bright red hair that betrayed their Celtic ancestry. This genetic trait gave my brothers and me the unusual condition of being born with blond hair on our heads that turned brown and beards that glowed red in adulthood. I may have to talk to God about this myself.

I can easily identify with the emotions Loani felt as I lost both of my brothers within a very short span of time. Elder Brother Bob, a 6'3" man of considerable proportions, whose storytelling, humor, hunting skills and kindness were legend, died from an unexpected heart attack at age 49. John, at 6'1" whose mechanical aptitude, motorcycle riding, firearm shooting and love of life were second to none, headed for the great beyond at the age of 47. In Light years, so to speak, folks considered me ancient at the age of 55. It seems that the brightest candles always burn out first.

Story #20: John's Wake

Brother John was not only my brother but also my best friend in life. His passing left a huge void at the depths of my soul. Like all brothers, we often argued and fought; however, there always was a bond that transcended the rancor.

Arguments are strange things. I have often remembered an argument I heard on television as talk show host Phil Donahue interviewed the Reverend Billy Graham's wife. Phil asked Mrs. Graham, "Do you and Billy ever fight?"

Mrs. Graham calmly answered a simple, "No."

The response resulted in a second challenge from Phil. "Do you mean you and Billy never fight?" he drilled.

"No, we have never fought," Mrs. Graham countered.

At this point Phil sported a disbelieving expression, looked into the camera and stated, "You mean you can tell all my millions of viewers that you and Billy have never had an argument in your entire lives?"

A dignified Mrs. Graham with absolute confidence continued, "Of course we argue. If we didn't, one of us would not be necessary."

It was clear to me that Phil Donahue did not have a clue that the word "fight" means a physical altercation, while the word "argue" implies an exchange of point and counterpoint aimed at reaching a higher level of collective knowledge.

Brother John and I were skilled at arguing, and our frequent exchanges drove bystanders crazy. To us it was great sport and learning.

John's death was lengthy as doctors struggled to understand the disease that slowly took away his motor controls. Towards the last, John was bedridden and speechless, but his body retained its strength. It was only the muscle controls that were missing.

It always puzzled me why the best-intentioned people I ever met could never seem to understand the silent communication that existed between John and me. During one of his last days on this earth, I entered his house, and upon seeing John in his elevated hospital bed, shouted, "Hey, do ya wanna arm wrestle." A home nurse, who was looking after John, stared daggers at me and chastised me for such a brash statement. She believed that my brother's mind was gone due to the ravages of the disease. I knew better.

As I approached the bed, John's left arm reached skyward and he rested it upon the bed rail. When he gripped my hand, the battle was joined and I was amazed at the strength and intensity of the struggle. John smiled.

John and I could communicate without language or gesture. My final communication with John occurred the night of his death. It was late in the evening and John was still struggling to survive. After visiting John's bedside, Mother and I had retired to the back porch of the old homestead, trying to relieve the tension. The silent communication from John had been clear. I looked at Mom and said, "We have to go home tonight. John won't die unless we leave." Mom sadly looked at me, and we left.

That night was the first good night of sleep I had in months. The next morning, I was notified of John's passing.

Following the funeral family and friends gathered at the old homestead for a wake. It was a celebration of John's life that most outsiders could not understand. Being a family of gunsmiths, doctors, nurses, engineers, farmers, shootists, bowyers, archers, outdoorsmen and hunters made it an odd affair. Especially when John's wife Ann suddenly stated, "I hate all of those pills John had to take. I wish I could blow them away." It was a good thought and we brought bottle after bottle of pills to the backyard shooting range. Annie picked up a rifle and began blasting the bottles from a hurriedly fabricated rail in front of the backstop.

My young children watched the activity with some confusion. They thought funerals were supposed to be sad affairs. Here was a large group of adults laughing and shooting and telling stories.

Mom leaned over to me and said, "You know, I wouldn't mind shooting a few of those bottles myself." I asked if she wanted me to get the 0.22-caliber Mossberg, and she responded, "Yes."

My children had no idea that their grandmother was an accomplished shootist. I loaded the rifle's clip with .22's and handed the rifle to Mom. She proceeded to fire four consecutive shots, each knocking over a filled bottom of pills and scattering their contents. My children stood in awe. I spoke to them saying, "You ought to see how well she shoots a bow. Now you know why we were always good boys."

-30-

Life is much too short to worry about the past, but it is excessively long not to remember the past and its lessons. These lessons are found in the stories. Life in Fort Jefferson resembled a carnival ride. Sometimes it was like a large lazy Ferris wheel, slowly rising and falling while the calliope of human music could be heard singing below. At other times, it was like a crazy tilt-o-wheel, darting from side to side and slamming you from one emotional elevation to another. It was the differences in our citizenry and the natural acceptance of these differences that made our community strong and viral.

Story #21: A Cold Start

Cladiss Birdsale was a large, raw-boned woman who had a heart larger than Texas. Cladiss lived in a comfortable home situated upon a small hill located diagonally across the county road from Mick Mong's general store.

Cladiss lived with her bed-ridden husband for most of her adult life. Her husband used to run a small store himself, but I once heard my father say, "He just gave up on life." I did not understand how anyone could just give up on life, but it did appear that Mr. Birdsale had. Some community children would "baby-sit" for Mr. Birdsale when Cladiss would have a need to go shopping, or just get away for a few hours. It was not a pleasant chore as Mr. Birdsale seldom talked, and even when he did it usually was a command to bring the bedpan. Sitting with Mr. Birdsale gave me a great respect for Cladiss and it taught me never to give up on life.

In the early 1950's Ft. Jefferson experienced a particularly cold winter with frequent sub-zero temperatures. My father looked out our front window early one frosty morning in time to see Cladiss trying to crank start her old Ford Model 'A' vehicle. The oil in the vehicle's crankcase was so cold that it was nearly impossible to turn the crank.

Dad was always a person to lend a helping hand, so he quickly threw on an old coat and rushed across the intersection to give Cladiss some assistance. Now you must remember that Dad was considered a "big man" in his day and he possessed ample upper body strength. Therefore, when he arrived at the scene, he told Cladiss to get into the Model

'A' and advance the spark and push on the accelerator pedal while he cranked the engine.

Dad threw all of his energies into the effort, but to outside observers it appeared that Dad was turning the crank in a bucket of frozen molasses. As if in slow motion, the circling crooked steel shaft gradually exhausted Dad's strength. As he stopped cranking to catch his breath, Cladiss hopped from the vehicle, told Dad to hop in, advance the spark, and push on the accelerator pedal.

What happened next should have been filmed, because only seeing is believing. As Dad did his assigned duty, Cladiss "womaned" the crank. With seemingly little effort, she spun the crank at a high velocity, but also yanked the front wheels of the Model 'A' off the ground on the up stroke of each revolution. Finally, the engine sputtered to life, coughing up a dark cloud of oil-contaminated gasoline fumes. Cladiss thanked Dad, hopped up into the vehicle and off to the big city Greenville she went. Dad merely shook his head from side to side and walked back to the house.

-30-

In reading the above story, I hope you understand why I have never understood the women's liberation movement. Cladiss, Summy, my mother and nearly all the women I knew in family and community seemed liberated to me. There were those folks in Fort Jefferson who chose to feel sorry for themselves, and to be subservient, but they were in the minority and of both genders. Frankly, as a small male child, most of the women I knew seemed very powerful and somewhat frightening.

Story #22: Happy New Year

It is an old tradition around the world to usher in a new year with celebration. Fort Jeffersonites maintained the old world customs and, quite literally, welcomed the New Year in with a bang.

It was a special time for us children because the bedtime curfew extended until one o'clock in the morning. There were smells associated with New Years Eve, especially the aroma of eggnog brewed with its nutmeg kicker. The highlight of the festivities came at the stroke of 12-midnight when men of the community would discharge large caliber firearms into the air. The weapons of choice were generally muzzle-loading shotguns. The guns were overcharged with black powder and then stuffed tightly with cloth patching to compress the powder in the barrel. Of course, no slug would be loaded into the barrel.

New Years Eve also was a time for family congregation, and our old homestead was a favorite. Our extended family was unusually close as my father's brother (the veterinarian) married my mother's sister. If that wasn't bad enough, my mother's two brothers (both farmers) married sisters. On most occasions, the farming side of the family would leave early. There really wasn't much to plant or harvest in Ohio on January 1, but there always was livestock that needed attention. My Dad and his brother, however, were professional men and had no problem staying up through the wee hours of the morning to welcome a new year.

Like most stories, this tale must take a side road at this junction. Living just to the south of the old homestead was a solitary old man called Charlie. A side yard separated our house from his by about 60 feet. Even into his later years, Charlie considered himself a lady's man. Once, while shopping at Claude and Summy's store, Charlie made an unwelcome advance to Summy. Summy responded by raising a meat cleaver over her head and explaining that she would split Charlie's skull if he advanced a step closer. He did not.

For a child, Charlie was the type man who conjured up images of buried treasures and skeletons in a basement. His yard was one where trespassing was forbidden and this law was honored, at least during daylight hours. It was a test of manhood to sneak through Charlie's yard and garden under the cover of darkness. To survive this passage was to cheat death. On one particular New Years Eve, I learned that Charlie's dark mystique not only affected children, but could have an effect on adults as well.

It was a very cold and still night as Dad and Uncle Dick prepared their muzzle-loading shotguns for the New Year blast. Their annual mission in life was to alert the remainder of the community that a new year had officially arrived. They meticulously measured the black powder charges and poured them into the double-barreled shotguns. They repeated old stories for the ears of the excited youth huddled around the activities. We learned where and how the guns were made, who had previously owned them and how it took a better marksman to follow through in the shot at a pheasant with a muzzle-loading shotgun than it did with a more modern center fire weapon. Long wooden ramrods then compressed cotton patches on top of the black powdered charges.

A double check was made on the time by tuning into a short wave radio station and all watches were synchronized to coordinated universal time. Tension and excitement rose as the clock approached the bewitching hour. I remember wondering what might happen if the New Year did not come. What if Dad and Dick's percussive welcome occurred at the wrong time? Would the New Year still begin or would it not?

A few minutes before the clock struck the magical hour, Dad and Uncle Dick bundled up, left the house with weapons in tow and took up positions between the homestead and Charlie's house. They thumbed the percussion caps onto their shotguns' nipples and then patiently waited for the second hand to drag its way around the clock face for the last agonizing minute. With 15 seconds remaining they, in unison, cocked the hammers and shouldered the firearms at a 45-degree angle into the air. 10-9-8-7-6-5-4-3-2-1------KaBooooommmmmmm!

The roar was deafening, but it was followed by a not so familiar or traditional tinkling sound that emanated from Charlie's house. The between-house concussion from the combined explosion of the four barrels of the two shotguns had shattered one of Charlie's large side windows. It was at this very moment that I learned that some adults also were leery of Charlie's eerie persona as my Uncle Dick fled the scene and headed for our house.

As it turned out, the New Year successfully was welcomed with a bang, like so many had been in the past. Dad explained to Charlie how the unfortunate mishap had occurred, and Charlie surprisingly seemed undisturbed as he continued his late night card game with friends. A plywood patch was applied to the shattered window until such time that a new glass pane could be installed by Dad.

It was a glorious beginning to a New Year, and one our family will never forget.

-30-

It strikes me that in today's legalistic America the last story would have a significantly different ending. Most likely a grand lawsuit would be initiated to punish the "guilty" and send a message to all society that adult safety locks should be placed on all firearms. The press would insinuate that all who use firearms are evil. A civil suit would be filed to extract monies to pay for all new windows on Charlie's house because the shock wave most likely did some unseen damage to the entire structure of the building. Charlie would have to be compensated for the damage done to his nervous system that might affect his concentration during future late-night card games. What a different picture children get today from so-called educated, kind, all-knowing and forgiving adults. The lessons I learned were far better. I learned that the grumpy old man living next door was not some evil ogre, and adults sometimes react like children under stressful situations. I also learned volumes about the power of concussive forces on physical structures. I used all of this knowledge, constructively, in later life. Children today learn that accidents should never happen, lawsuits are God's blessing on humanity, one should always point a finger of blame and forgiveness is a fool's folly. How foolish!

Story #23: Over the Edge

It was Spring when my Brother Bob paid a visit to the Army and Navy Store located out of the downtown district in Greenville. The Army and Navy Store was a mystical place for young men. The building that housed the establishment looked more like a church than a store. It was filled to the brim with old military equipment, all of which looked like something that any self-respecting young patriot should own.

As mentioned in a previous story, my Brother Bob had a great imagination and could see possibilities where others only saw obstacles. During this visit to the Army and Navy Store, Bob happened upon a wonderful device and its cost was a great bargain that fell within his limited financial resources. It was a flare parachute. For those of you who have no knowledge about such things, the United States Army sometimes likes to illuminate a night battlefield so that bad situations can be seen. To accomplish this end, from airplanes it drops large incendiary devices that slowly float to the ground under the umbrella-like canopy of a parachute. Some of the flares they carried could weigh over 100 pounds, which was close to the weight of Brother Bob.

When Bob brought the nylon fabric and line contraption home, it didn't take long for the Light Brothers to fabricate a harness into which a human could strap himself. Being Spring, strong breezes frequently blew through Fort Jefferson and for several days we would carry the parachute to an appropriate location, strap on the harness then wait for a gust of wind to inflate the chute and drag us across the yard. It was during one of these drags that Brother Bob came up with another great idea which involved great height and courage.

You may recall that American Aggregates owned a gravel pit that rested a short distance from Fort Jefferson. One of these pits had a particularly high cliff that jutted up about 50 feet above a crystal-blue pond. Bob figured that parachutes were for dropping people to the ground, not dragging them over it.

Now the Light Brothers weren't geniuses, but we knew that we would not be able to bundle the parachute in such a way that it could open in only a 50-foot drop. As usual, Bob had a solution. He figured that John and I could run behind him carrying the parachute. Bob would then launch himself off the cliff, and we would throw the parachute into the air behind him. It sounded like a great idea to John and me. Of course, we weren't jumping off the cliff.

It was Saturday morning when we arrived at the pit. We made a quick check about the property to make sure no weekend workers were on the site; then, we quickly unloaded our equipment and headed for the gravel precipice. Bob strapped on the harness about 30 feet from the edge of the abyss. We then talked over last minute assignments. Off we flew, hell bent for leather.

Bob yelled something as he leapt with all of his strength from the crag. I have no idea what he yelled as I was much too worried about throwing the parachute and stopping before I tumbled over the edge. Unfortunately for Bob, John and I stopped a few feet short of the edge, causing the parachute to be dragged through the grass. Also, more unfortunately for Bob, the wind was blowing towards the rock face, so when the parachute inflated, it was pushed by the wind against the rock face.

I don't know if you can imagine being in Bob's shoes. As he hurtled towards the water below, he was repeatedly bounced against the pit's rock face. From John's and my viewport, he looked a lot like Wiley Coyote from a scene out of a Roadrunner cartoon. It's amazing how the sights, sounds and smells of such an incident stay with you for life. My guess is that Bob's memories were even more vivid than mine.

Bob eventually hit the water below with a "katoosh" sound that seemed like the period below an exclamation point at the end of an exciting sentence.

"you okay?" John yelled.

"Yowl!" Bob grunted back, as if trying to convince himself that all of his body parts were still attached and in the right positions.

Grandma Z used to say, "God protects foolish children." It's just amazing to me how wise she was.

After a brief discussion at the bottom of the pit, Bob decided that one jump was just the right number. We rolled up the parachute and headed back to the homestead. It was a very quiet ride.

-30-

Such adventures are great training grounds, especially if you live through them. For some reason, certain sects of our society have decided that all accidents can be prevented through legislation. God, through Moses, provided 10 simple laws by which mankind can live a good and rightous life. By the time Jesus walked on the earth, I have been told that the Jewish people had about 600,000 laws on their books. One of these laws made it illegal to drag a chair across the dirt floor of a home on the Sabbath as it was considered plowing. Seems to me that sometimes it is far better to trust in the laws of God and chance rather than man-made laws. I doubt very much that God cares about someone dragging a chair across the floor at anytime. Well-meaning people occasionally frighten me.

In 1957, our immediate family grew by one with the arrival of Jane Grace. Jane came into the world to meet three older brothers, who were settled in their ways and had no idea what to expect from a sister. She was a methodical child with curly light blonde hair and light blue eyes. Jane was a welcomed addition. Dad had received a precious jewel and Mom finally had someone with whom to share feminine thoughts.

Story #24: She Didn't Hear That From Me

It was Jane's second birthday. Two years of age in the Light family was the first time when children fully recognized that their birthday was a special day for them alone.

For Jane to have survived two years was somewhat of a miracle in itself. On numerous occasions, she was treated more like a football than a baby girl. Nevertheless, there she was, sitting in the middle of the living room floor, surrounded by family and presents.

A large package adorned with shiny wrapping paper and perfectly placed ribbons and bows was slid in front of Jane's folded legs. With great care and precision, Jane began to apply her considerable knowledge and strength to free the package from its gaudy bonds. Her tiny fingers pinched, pulled, tugged, and squeezed. The expression on her face showed intensity never witnessed in the past. The battle continued for many minutes when, suddenly Jane paused, and she quietly, but determinedly, stated, "Shit!"

Without hesitation, Mom interrupted the spontaneous laughter with, "She didn't hear that from me!" Of course, my brothers and I never admitted to uttering such vulgarity in the presence of innocence.

-30-

Jane grew up quickly, both in size and intellect. She adapted well to the family environment where shooting guns and bows was as natural as walking. Jane competed on an equal par with the boys and maintained her femininity.

Collection #2:

Canvas: Westward Ho

Setting: 1949-1952: World War II was over, but tensions around the world were still high. Communism had gained great favor in the east and in 1950 things were about to erupt in the small country of Korea. Industry in the United States was busy rebuilding Europe. Gasoline rationing was a thing of the past, and technologies were growing at an exponential rate. The strength of the economy allowed Americans to be more mobile and adventuresome.

Fort Jefferson's economic condition was still in good shape, and both the Shaffer and Mick Mong's country stores were faring well, and pumping more gasoline than ever. General George still painted his bicycle every week and Shorty Longfellow still furnished dynamite for the grand spring opening of bass season at Wayne Lakes Park. Granddad Light continued to manage the park, and he insured that the fish hatchery's rearing ponds were producing quality game fish to be shipped around the country.

Dad worked as an aircraft research engineer at General Motors Aeroproducts Division in Vandalia, Ohio. In 1950, he was working on hydraulic system designs for the top-secret F84-F fighter jet. Since the center of the world for jet aircraft research was California, Dad packed up the family and the Light Tribe headed west. My two brothers and I made the journey in the back seat of the Buick. Our traveling companion was Dad's fellow engineer, Roy Brandes, his wife, Ruth, and their young daughter, Patty. Roy and family became life-long friends and part of the extended Light family of outdoorsmen.

After an eventful journey, we landed in Burbank, California. After a yearlong stay, we returned to Fort Jefferson, only to return to California in 1952. During this trip, we lived in Mojave while dad and fellow engineers tested the then completed F84-F at Muroc (later to be known as Edwards Air Force Base). At the time, downtown Mojave was three blocks long and it sported thirteen bars, McClusky, the local sheriff, packed twin Colt .45 revolvers, and every Saturday night, truck loads of MP's and AP's (military police) invaded town to quell the many disturbances. It was an exciting time in history.

Chapter #6: California Dreamin'

It is hard to put into words what goes through a 3-year-old boy's mind at any time, but it is even harder to imagine what goes through a 3-year-old cowboy-wannabe's mind when he learns he is heading to the Wild West. Some folks say that they cannot remember when they were 3 years of age. Perhaps, they just did not yet have well developed imaginations. What I remember most about the journey west was a confliction over whether to dress as an Indian or a cowboy. Lord knows, I did not want to come upon a tribe of hostiles dressed as a cowboy. On the other hand, it was my understanding that some cowboys did not treat Indians very well. One thing for sure, a part of Fort Jefferson, Ohio, traveled with us to the promised land of sun and fun.

Story #25: Along the Way

Writers have long recorded that pioneers, who risked their lives and all of their worldly possessions to sail across the endless plains in cloth-covered wagons and climb over the great divide, had boundless courage. Our journey west in the old Buick may pale in comparison; nevertheless, since I have had time to raise three children of my own, I believe that my parents were extremely courageous to load up Grandma Z, my two brothers and me in one vehicle, and head west. Three young boys in the back seat of a Buick can be a very frightening thing.

The Light-Brandes two-car caravan headed west in December 1949. When we made our first stop in Missouri, Roy walked up to Dad and said, "Jim, people are going to be able to track us all the way to California if your boys keep throwing all those Kleenex out the windows." It was not as if my brothers and I were littering. There was a lot to be learned about aerodynamics when one observed the flight of a tissue in high-velocity winds.

As we passed through Oklahoma, we stopped along the road beside a giant tree where we ate lunch. Oklahoma had been hit hard by the Great Depression in the 1930's, and it took many years for families living there to recover. The demeaning word "Okees" was coined by more well-to-do folks to describe those unfortunate Oklahoma souls who wore any clothing they could borrow or buy.

Our rag-tag caravan would not have made the cover of a fashion magazine as we munched down our sandwiches that had been packed in paper grocery bags. I was suffering from an ear infection and had an Indian headdress wrapped around my head that looked like a turban. My brothers and I each were bundled up in a couple layers of shirts or sweaters. Baggy blue jeans completed the ensemble. Patty wasn't dressed much better.

Traffic was light on the two-lane road, so we all took notice when a car slowed down as it approached our location. As the car rolled by slowly, a woman, sitting on the passenger side of the vehicle with her window rolled down, yelled at her husband saying, "Look Harold! Okees!"

Mom and Ruth looked shocked, while Dad and Roy broke out in a well-deserved laugh.

My brothers and I frequently practiced our wrestling skills in the back seat arena, so for the sake of my parent's sanity, I sometimes was farmed out to the Brandes car to keep Patty company. Patty was at a stage in her young life where she called every other child "Peeboo Face." She never said this phrase just once. Patty would look you straight in one eye and chant, "Peeboo Face, Peeboo Face, Peeboo Face!" I was never sure exactly what the name meant, but I did know that I did not like the look on Patty's face when she would

use the term on me. Things were even worse when I made the mistake of telling my brothers about the nickname. From that time on, anytime my brothers chose to raise my blood pressure, they would resort to the same name-calling. Peeboo Face was a phrase that would live in infamy – at least in my mind.

The farther west we traveled, the harder it was to find drinking water, and gas stations were few and far between. Dad purchased a canvas bag that he filled with water, and then tied it securely in front of the Buick's radiator. The bag was somewhat porous to allow moisture to seep to the surface where the evaporation process would cool the water in the bag. This was particularly useful when we traversed desolate Death Valley.

It seemed like we passed through endless flat land for days. My first real memory of believing I was in cowboy and Indian country came when I saw magnificent mountains appear on the horizon. At first, they appeared like clouds, but as we got closer, it was clear to see that they were actual mountains jutting up to the sky. Sleeping had been common during the Great Plains portion of the journey, but mountain travel held adventure at every turn. In those days there were few if any guardrails along the roadway, so a mistake could mean a fatal plunge for hundreds of feet. It was not unusual to see the rusted carcass of an old vehicle lying in a craggy valley, far below the highway. Grandma Z was not thrilled about the ride through the mountains, and, in fact, she consumed an entire bottle of aspirin as we traversed the range.

I remember well when we headed down the west side of the mountains and eventually saw Los Angeles in the distance. We stopped to see the massive wooden aqueduct that carried water from the mountains down to the cities along the coast. It was the largest manmade structure I had ever seen.

Eventually, we arrived at our new home in Burbank, a suburb located just north of Los Angeles. Our new house was everything our Fort Jefferson home was not. Our Burbank house was only one-story tall and it had a fireplace in the living room. It also had a television that we all could crowd around and watch several stations that scheduled a variety of entertaining shows. There were even cowboy and Indian shows, and for some inexplicable reason, they seemed even more realistic than they did in Ohio.

It was not a far drive for Dad to reach his new worksite, a high-tech Quonset building where engineers were creating designs for the new Republic F84F jet aircraft.

Perhaps the most exciting thing of all for a three-year-old country boy was the Good Humor Man. The Good Humor Man piloted a small, white, three-wheeled vehicle that held a variety of ice cream treasures. Calliope-like music emitted from the little vehicle as it patrolled the neighborhoods day after day, seeking out enthusiastic children who would rush to the street, dragging their parents or grandparents with them. One day my neighbor and friend Phillip, who was my age, frantically ran out of his house as the Good Humor Man was passing. Seeing Phillip in his rearview mirror at the very last minute, the Good Humor Man slammed on the brakes and came to a screeching halt in the middle of the street. Phillip then yelled, "Not today, but maybe tomorrow."

"Could heaven possibly be a better place," I wondered.

Being only three years of age limited my exposure to this grand new world called California. Dad and Mom did have time to take us on many excursions, including my first encounter with an ocean at a beach in Santa Barbara. However, on some occasions the adults were able to break free of the juvenile reins while the children remained home with Grandma Z. And, this brings us to the next story.

Story #26: Horsing Around

In 1942, the beautiful Santa Anita Park thoroughbred horse track, which had been in operation since 1934, was closed and then converted by the U.S. government to a Japanese Assembly Center. Later, it became a U.S. Army base known as Camp Santa Anita. The park opened for horse racing again in 1945. By the time the Light clan arrived in Burbank, the park was in full swing.

Dad and mom, along with friends and family, decided to spend a day of relaxation at the track during the family's 1950 stay in California. It was a typical California day – beautiful.

Dad and Mom weren't particularly prone to gambling, but throughout the day, all of the participants played the horses with conservative betting. By the time the last race of the day was called to the post, no singular person in the group had enough cash to place a viable bet. They all decided they would pool their remaining cash and make one final bet in the last race.

There was an animated discussion as each person had his own idea which horse would have the best chance. A decision was reached after the hurried debate. It was a consensus-based decision based on science and understanding. Engineering also played a role and Dad, his friend and his nephew Jimmy Kessler all were research engineers. It was decided that Jimmy, the youngest of the clan, would carry the pooled financial resources to the windows to place the bet. Unfortunately, Jimmy not only was the youngest of the clan, but also the member who had sipped the most beer during the afternoon of festivities.

Jim - Goat or Hero?

The horses were called to the post, but Jimmy had not yet returned from the betting window. All were concerned, not particularly about the health or whereabouts of Jimmy, rather whether or not the bet on the sure-to-win horse had been placed.

Seconds before the gates loosed the thoroughbreds, Jimmy ambled back.

"Where have you been?" someone shouted.

"Just placing the bet," he answered.

Then, someone looked at the ticket.

"You bet on the wrong horse," they yelled in unison.

At the same instant, the race was on.

Family and friends were busily chastising Jimmy as the race continued. It was not a friendly situation. As the horses were coming around the final turn, the track announcer was shouting with excitement. The name of the *leading horse was not the horse the group had selected to win. At the same time, someone noticed the name of the horse on the ticket Jimmy had purchased sounded like the name being broadcast by the announcer.*

In an instant, they all began screaming at the horses and not Jimmy. In addition, the horse on the ticket not only won the race but also won against huge odds.

The group's winnings were adequate to treat everyone to a fancy meal at one of Los Angeles' finest restaurants. It was a day to remember, especially for Jimmy, who went from goat to hero in a New York second.

-30-

Jimmy Kessler and his wonderful wife Joann were two of my favorite cousins. Both were graduates of Ohio State University – Jimmy in engineering and Joann in pharmacy. Later they set up housekeeping in a place they cheerfully named Protestant Hill, located just outside of Ogden, Utah. As I grew older, so did my love and respect for them. When I left home in 1965 to tour the country with a traveling road band, I had the opportunity to visit the Kessler's in California. Jimmy took me on a tour of the old stomping grounds where I learned that my father's high-tech research lab had been converted into a place where eucalyptus trees were sold.

Chapter #7: Mojave – Home in the Desert

Later, in 1950, our family moved away from Burbank, and spent one year back at our Ohio homestead before packing up and heading west a second time in 1952. This time the destination was a god-forsaken town called Mojave, which sat a few miles from Muroc, our nation's top-secret research test facility for aircraft development. Our place of residence was in a small motel that was equipped with one bedroom, one living area, one bathroom and one kitchen. The railroad had a station in Mojave, and the town was constantly permeated with the pungent aroma of diesel fuel.

Mojave was situated near another small town called Tehachapi. Between the two "cities" sat the spacious desert ranch of movie star Will Rogers, Jr. To the east of Mojave were mountains, and to the west of Mojave stretched endless miles of parched desert. During the daylight hours, frequently the temperature peaked over 100°F with winds coming from the west. At night, cool winds would race down the mountainsides from the east and temperatures would routinely fall to 40°F.

The 13 bars in the three-block downtown area served as magnets that attracted servicemen and many of United States' most-wanted felons. Local Native American children would frequent the town's only movie theater in which they would practice their wood carving skills on the armrests of the theater seating. Since their families made livings by herding sheep, the theater smelled like many of the barnyards I had visited with my Uncle Dick, the veterinarian.

The town and surrounding area was patrolled by Sheriff McClusky and one solitary State Highway Patrolman named Stan Allen. There were rattlesnakes, jackrabbits, roadrunners and all sorts of critters – both human and animal. It was a wonderful playground for three young boys. It also was a place where risk was common, but, at times, unexpected.

Story #27: The Great Shake

Things in and around Mojave on July 20, 1952, were a little strange. All of the animals sensed something that we humans could not see, hear, touch, taste or smell. That evening, those people who had pet dogs and cats were forced to let their animals go outside, because the animals seemed nervous and at times frantic. When released, the dogs and cats fled the area.

A local dairy farmer, who every night allowed his cows to remain in the barn for warmth and security, was astounded when his cows began frantically kicking at the wooden-plank walls. When the farmer opened the sliding door to the barn, the cattle stampeded out and fled into the field, where they promptly separated and bedded down, seemingly at peace.

Another area resident called his veterinarian and requested that the vet come to his ranch. For many years, the man had watched each evening as his pet peacock flew to its perch atop an abandoned windmill. For some inexplicable reason, that evening the peacock huddled on the ground. When the rancher carried the peacock up to the top of the windmill, the peacock immediately flew back to terra firma and again huddled on the ground. The veterinarian had no explanation for the abnormal behavior.

Nothing seemed out of line in our small motel abode. We had our evening meal and my brothers and I ate off our chair-turned table.

Later we played a few card games, and then retired for the night. My two brothers and I all bunked in one foldout bed in the living area. Mom and Dad slept in the dwelling's solitary bedroom.

At precisely 4:52 a.m. the next morning, our perception of the world, and the existences of many other Californians, changed. For 14 area residents the change was permanent. It was at this exact time that one of the largest earthquakes to strike California rocked the area surrounding Mojave and Tehachapi at a level of 7.7 on the Richter scale. The estimated damage was $50,000,000.

Mom and Dad awoke as the bed in which they were sleeping began to bounce up and down violently. When Mom attempted to get out of bed, the motel room shifted about 18 inches off its foundation, and the bedroom wall struck mom, knocking her back into the bed. The quake did not last long, and luckily for us, our little motel home-away-from-home was constructed of reinforced concrete, and that allowed it to withstand the assault. Others were not so lucky. My brothers and I slept through the initial quake, but we felt the numerous after shocks for many days following the main jolt.

Our Earthquake Proof Home

The epicenter of the quake ran right though the middle of the Will Rogers, Jr. ranch, where the ground split open along a fault that shifted in elevation by four feet. Tehachapi was severely damaged and lives were lost. The next day, Dad decided to take us on a trip to Tehachapi to witness the carnage there.

It was a bright and sunny day as we traversed the desert highway in our big Buick. All seemed well until my father suddenly uttered, "What the hell?" As we all stared through the windshield, we became mesmerized. On one side of the road was a row of electric power poles. On the other side of the road were telephone poles. Off in the distance we could see one pair of poles after another rock back and forth violently. Even worse, the pairs of poles being shaken were approaching our vehicle at an alarming rate. As we continued, we saw a wave extending away from both sides of the road as far as the eye could see across the flat desert. The wave was about three feet tall and was gentle enough that as it moved, it did not fracture the asphalt surface of the road. Soon we drove over the wave, at which time we all quickly reversed our view, and watched the wave as it continued on its way, eventually vanishing from sight.

Arriving at Tehachapi, we were shocked to see an entire external wall of the town's main hotel had fallen away, exposing what resembled a giant dollhouse.

The downtown area looked like a war zone. The four support legs holding the town's water tower had separated from the giant steel ball that contained thousands of gallons of water. The sphere fell to the ground, split open and expelled all of its water in one split second. The wall of water picked up a new Ford pickup truck and neatly wrapped the truck around a telephone pole – bumper to bumper – without scratching the vehicle's paint. One entire family died when the building in which they resided collapsed around them.

The main railroad line that carried supplies from the east to the west coast was completely severed by the quake. At Tehachapi Pass, a series of railroad tunnels were carved through the mountains. It had been a major engineering feat and at one location, long trains navigated an inclined circle that was so tight the trains would actually run over themselves as they traversed the labyrinth. Unfortunately, several of the tunnels collapsed during the quake. Earth moving equipment *arrived from several states to, quite literally, move a mountain in order to restore rail service in the shortest possible time. The massive operation continued for 24 hours per day, 7 days per week for many months, and slowly the mountain that contained Tehachapi Pass was reduced to a flat plain over which the trains could travel.*

As we drove back to Mojave, we all were overwhelmed by the destructive power of nature, and the earthquake shook our confidence in California's stability. However, our faith in the wisdom of God was greatly enhanced because we noticed that all of the neighborhood animals had returned to their homes unscathed. Even the peacock, we later learned, had returned to its perch the next night.

-30-

For weeks following the record earthquake, we became nervous when our living room floor lamp would begin to wobble as if possessed by a demon. Next, the dishes in the kitchen would begin to clatter, as the intensity of the after shocks would increase. After a time it all seemed normal, as did some of the many other peculiarities of our western adventure, as you will see in the following stories.

Story #28: Stan and the Gold Queen Mine

Stan Allen and his lovely wife, Ruth, became best friends with my parents. Stan was a California Highway Patrolman who patrolled the vast desert regions and helped keep the peace in Mojave, especially during the rowdy Friday and Saturday nights when airmen and soldiers invaded town to celebrate.

Stan and Dad had a mutual love of firearms and human nature. Both enjoyed patrolling in the squad car together on evenings and weekends.

Like most highway patrolmen, Stan had witnessed his fair share of horrendous accidents that claimed the lives of young and old indiscriminately. He also was aware that many of these accidents were caused by drunk drivers. Stan had his own way of dealing with drunk drivers that both solved the problem and saved the State much in court costs. When Stan would stop an inebriated foe at night, he would take the driver's car keys and throw them into the desert. "When you are sober enough to find your keys, you will be sober enough to drive home," Stan would advise.

At this time, I must explain a little history of the region. The Gold Queen Mine sat in the Soledad Mountains, located a short distance southwest of Mojave. Millions of dollars of gold were taken from this historic mine; consequently, security was always critical, especially during the war years.

One cool desert night, Stan was on routine patrol when he stopped a vehicle that was drifting across the centerline. When he approached the vehicle, he saw a very intoxicated, middle age man behind the wheel. Stan gave the man his usual sermon, removed the car keys from the man's hand, and pitched them into the desert. It was a routine bust. At least, that is what Stan thought at the time.

The next morning, Stan was awakened by a ringing telephone. When he answered, he was greeted by the hostile voice of one of his superiors.

"Did you stop a drunk driver last night in the desert?" Stan was asked.

"Sure," Stan replied, "several."

"Did you throw a set of keys into the desert?" the boss shouted.

"Uh, yes," Stan responded.

"Well," the commander added, "That guy was the Gold Queen Mine foremen and they haven't been able to open the mine today because he was the only guy with the keys. It's costing millions of dollars!"

-30-

Stan's "secret weapon" was no longer a secret, and Stan never again used it during his private war against crime and drunk drivers. Policing a town like Mojave was an art form. It required an attitude that probably would not be tolerated today. In all respects, Mojave was the Wild West, and it sometimes took a real cowboy to keep things under control. One of these cowboys was Sheriff McClusky.

Story #29: McClusky

I don't remember much about the sheriff that patrolled the streets of Mojave in 1952. What I do remember will likely sound like a tale out of the 1800's. McClusky was not a big man. He was short and stout. He had steely blue eyes that could stare a grizzly bear down in a smile contest. When doing his duty as an officer of the law, he strapped on twin holsters that carried twin Colt 45-caliber revolvers, and he carried a sawed-off shotgun in the front seat of his cruiser.

Dad met McClusky through Dad's association with Stan Allen. Consequently, at times Dad would ride with McClusky on evenings and weekends as McClusky patrolled the bar areas.

At one time, many believed that four of the FBI's 10 most wanted list were living in the Mojave area. It was not yet a tame town, especially on the weekends.

Dad once asked McClusky why he always carried a sawed-off, 12-gage shotgun when he entered a bar. McClusky responded saying, "Jim, those guys would laugh at a pistol because they know they could still get to you and kill you before they would die. They all respect a shotgun."

One night, while patrolling, McClusky explained that he was on the lookout for one particular felon. McClusky saw the villain's car parked in front of one of the town's 13 bars. McClusky parked the cruiser two cars behind the suspect vehicle and waited.

A few minutes later, the felon and his girl friend exited the bar. McClusky told Dad to stay in the patrol car, and then McClusky hopped from the cruiser and approached the suspects. As McClusky confronted the male suspect, Dad saw the girl friend pull a pistol from her purse. Dad leaped from the car, but by the time he traversed the two-car length, McClusky had reached across the hood of the car, drug the woman across the hood, handcuffed both subjects, and was standing with a foot on the necks of each while holding a Colt pistol in each hand.

"If you sons a bitches try that again, I'll kill both of you," McClusky promised.

-30-

There are those today who will tell you that the previous story demonstrates barbaric behavior on the part of a peace officer. In my view, the judges and attorneys in the United States today closely mimic ancient rulers and priests whose self-righteousness and isolated elitism drove them to force their personal values onto the masses in order to control the masses. Rulers and priests have repeated these mistakes throughout history in the name of civilization; however, the civilizations that made these mistakes in the past are no longer in existence. Most of the McClusky-like policemen have been killed – some figuratively and some physically – by the actions of our legalistic ardor. A bell of sadness will toll when the final "McClusky" is eliminated, for the bell will be the harbinger of a very dangerous world.

Story #30: Characters

Brother Bob was 12 years old and far worldlier than I was by the time we settled in Mojave. Bob, while exploring the limited back alleys in town, discovered Wesley. Wesley was one of those guys who probably looked 40 years of age when he turned 16. Bob discovered Wesley sitting on a rickety wooden chair in front of his trailer-like place of abode. Wesley had a gnarly face that looked like the parched desert ravines.

"Where do you hail from?" Wesley mumbled as Bob walked by.

"Ohio, a little place called Fort Jefferson," Bob answered.

"A fort huh! What the hell kind of fort did they ever have in Ohio?" Wesley said as he flicked the ashes off the end of his hand-rolled cigarette.

"A supply fort for Fort Greenville," Bob blurted out in a defensive manner.

"I thought Greenville was in South Carolina," Wesley responded in a way that seemed as if he was testing Bob for some sacrificial rite.

You must remember that Bob, later in life, earned Eagle Scout status in the Boy Scouts of America, and he was no dummy when it came to the knowledge of history, especially the history of Greenville and Darke County, Ohio.

"Yes and no," Bob replied. "There is a Greenville in about every state, but my Greenville is located in southwestern Ohio, and Annie Oakley came from there."

"My name's Wesley," the grizzled codger explained, "But, my friends call me Wes."

It was at this time that Wes pulled out a large fixed-blade knife and started carving dirt from under his fingernails.

"I's got a bit of knowledge about forts and such. I done a lot of work in the movies, throwin' knives and such. Don't work much anymore."

Bob was hooked.

"You were in the movies, Wes?"

"Yep. Worked with Tom Mix and all those guys. I got to stick em with my knives," Wes explained.

"You threw knives at them?" Bob questioned with a puzzled look on his face.

"Yep. Had to stick em in the back or in the chest. Never so much as cut a one of em. Don't do that no more," Wes added.

"How did ya stick them without cutting them," Bob quizzed.

"They wore vests of wood glued to steel under their shirts," Wes explained. The knives stick in the wood but don't go through the steel. The tough shots were when they rode by on horses," He added.

Wes stood up and walked to his house. When he returned he was carrying a hand full of knives and a box of kitchen matches. Wes laid the knives on the ground by his chair, then meticulously began to stick matches into the ground along the edge of the concrete sidewalk. He returned to his chair, sat down, bent over and picked up the knives.

"Wanna learn how to throw knives," Wes offered.

"Sure!" Bob said without hesitation.

With this acknowledgement, Wes began to throw the knives at the kitchen matches. With each knife thrown, one match would burst into flame, until all of the matches were burning, and all of the knives were thrown. For weeks, it was a common occurrence to see the Light brothers gathering around a very talented and strange old man who amazed us with his wit and skill.

Wes was only one of numerous unusual characters who lived in Mojave in 1952. One day as 9-year-old brother John was walking down the street upon where our motel and Stan and Ruth Allen's house were located, a middle-aged woman, wearing baggy blue jeans, a heavy jacket, and a sock hat upon her head despite the 90+ ° temperatures, ran out to the sidewalk and pinched John's nose between her fingers. Then she began yelling obscenities at John while he squirmed in an attempt to get free of the powerful grip. Ruth Allen heard the noise and ran to John's rescue.

That evening when Ruth's state-highway-patrolman husband returned home, she informed him of the weird incident. Stan went to a local bar and saw the odd-looking woman sitting with a man at the bar. She was still wearing the bagging blue jeans, the heavy jacket and the sock hat. When the woman walked away from the man and headed for the restroom, Stan ambled up to the bar and questioned the man. Stan asked, "Do you know that woman well?"

"Nope, I just met her a little while ago," came the response.

"Doesn't she seem a bit odd to you, what with the coat and hat – especially when it is about 90 degrees in here?" Stan probed.

Stan was astounded when the man shook his head from side to side and answered, "Nah, she doesn't seem unusual to me."

-30-

Over the years, I have learned that "unusual" is in the eyes and mind of the beholder. From my youthful position, the crazy woman down the street was a threat to be avoided, but to the man in the bar, she was a delight to behold. Perspective is a complex concept.

Story #31: Desert Swimming

To say that there was not much water to be found around Mojave would be overstating the obvious. The town had one small swimming pool that was situated in the public school building, but water sports in the area were not destined to be a tourist draw. For a family that was raised near Wayne Lakes Park where small lakes were plentiful and streams flowed to and fro, the Mojave desert was a strange and mystical place.

When my brothers and I first visited the local swimming pool, I was not allowed to swim in the deep end of the pool or jump from the diving board due to a rule that said swimmers must swim the length of the pool and back to prove their abilities.

When we returned to the motel following the swim, my brothers explained to Dad that I was not allowed to dive from the board. Dad looked me in the eye and asked, "Can't you swim back and forth?"

"Underwater I can," I said.

Dad looked at my brothers and asked, "Did the rule say that he had to swim back and forth on top of the water?"

Both brothers shrugged their shoulders.

The next day, Dad walked us to the pool and immediately went to the lifeguard and posed the question, "Does it say in the rules that my son must swim back and forth the length of the pool ON TOP of the water?"

The lifeguard looked dumbfounded. "I guess not," he said quietly.

"Go ahead," Dad smiled as he motioned me to dive into the pool.

I complied and passed the test by swimming the two pool lengths under the water. The lifeguard nodded to Dad, Dad left and I was allowed to go off the diving board. I felt 10 feet tall.

Generally, the Light tribe had always gone swimming in lakes, not pools. It was always more fun as the scenery was better under the water. Dad was determined to find a place near Mohave where we could picnic and go swimming. Finally, he decided to take us to a place on the map called Oak Creek.

When we reached the site, there was a stream flowing through the desert in a shallow ravine, and the stream was bordered with a few sparely spaced trees. The maximum depth of the stream was about three inches.

It's very hard to explain how anyone could possibly swim in two inches of water, but the Light's and Allen's did exactly that. Brother Bob was bored with the swimming and decided to chase gophers, which were in abundance around the stream.

Bob had left our sight for only a few minutes when suddenly his voice broke the relative calm.

"Dad, Dad, hey Dad," he yelled. "Come here. Hurry! There's a big rattlesnake that just ate my gopher."

Bob had been chasing a gopher when it darted down a hole in the dusty ground. Bob ran to the hole and thought about putting his foot into the hole in an attempt to scare the *gopher out the other end of the tunnel. A premonition told him not to place his foot in the hole, and when he peered into the abyss, there lay a four-foot long rattlesnake, all coiled to strike.*

Dad inspected the scene, and then returned to the family car to procure his bow and one arrow. A single shot pierced the snake's head, and the snake's body was ceremoniously dragged from the hole and put on display. Sure enough, about one third of the way down the snake's body was a large swelling that contained the freshly swallowed body of the gopher Bob had been chasing.

As officer Stan gazed at the rattlesnake, he calmly reached to his side and stroked his 38-caliber revolver then said, "Jim, wouldn't it have been easier with this?"

Dad said, "Nope," and the entourage returned to the stream to watch the young swimmers,

-30-

If you are naturally curious, you will probably be happy to know that rattlesnake truly does taste a lot like chicken.

Story #32: UFO's – Fact or Fiction

Dad never talked much around the house about his work. We all knew that he was working on a jet aircraft, and occasionally, a pilot or another engineer would visit our motel home. For example, on one occasion, the first pilot to break the infamous sound barrier, Chuck Yeager, stopped by to say hello. At that time and place, Chuck was not the celebrity he was to become in later years.

One evening, Dad was unusually quiet when he returned home from the base.

"What happened?" Mom asked.

"A couple of the guys said they saw two UFO's today," Dad responded.

A test pilot and the chase plane pilot were flying their jets in formation over the desert while the engineers were gathered in a hanger, listening to the radio chatter between the tower and the planes in case trouble was reported.

Suddenly, one of the pilots reported seeing two strange disk-shaped objects flying in formation with the jets. The chatter rippled with excitement. The pilots described two unidentified objects shadowing each maneuver the jets made, except that the disks appeared to move only in right angles, not the smooth curves that the jets traversed. The encounter lasted several minutes, and the pilots were instructed to return to the base.

When the two jets taxied back to the hanger, the engineers gathered around the pilots to hear firsthand what *had happened. A loud announcement over the hanger's public address system interrupted the animated conversations.*

The control tower brass summoned the two pilots to the tower for debriefing immediately. When the pilots returned to the hanger some time later, they stated they were ordered not to discuss their encounter with anyone on or off base, or their jobs would be in jeopardy.

-30-

This singular UFO incident kindled in me a curiosity that continues to the present. Shortly before my father died at age 60, I asked him if he believed the unidentified flying objects came from outer space or if they were man made. He explained that he had mixed feelings over the years, but believed, most likely, the vehicles were earthly creations of unknown origin. One actual "flying saucer" was tested at Edwards Air Force Base during the 1950's. It was the Avrocar. (Shown at right). The complex and innovative craft actually was flown, but it never achieved its promises. Test pilots were instrumental in the successful development of high performance aircraft, and these pilots were a remarkable breed of men, as can be witnessed in the next two stories.

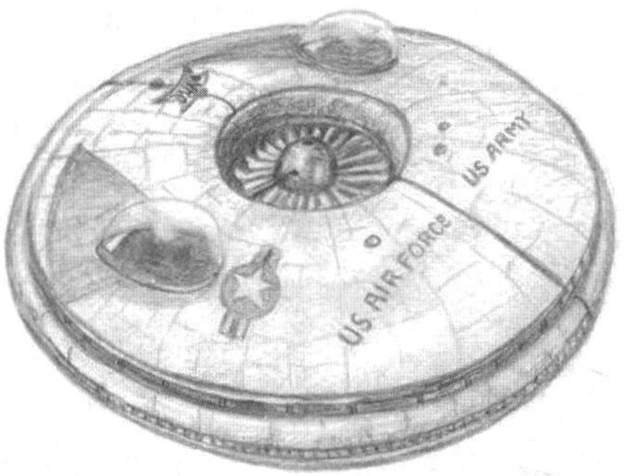

Story #33: Lucky

Lucky was a test pilot and a good friend of my father. Lucky earned his nickname when a design flaw in an experimental airplane caused a catastrophic failure that nearly claimed his life.

It was a typical day over Muroc as Lucky guided his test aircraft up and up into the deep blue sky. It was a particularly dangerous day because he was about to embark on one of the highest risk maneuvers that all new planes were forced to endure – the infamous full-power dive.

For those of you not familiar with aircraft testing, the full-power dive occurs when a plane is taken to a significant altitude, and then the pilot stands the plane on its nose and thrusts the throttle to full. The airplane hurtles towards the ground at ever-increasing velocity until a designated test speed is reached. At this point, the pilot pulls back on the control stick in order to put the craft under ultra-high dynamic loading as it strains to return to level flight.

All was going well until Lucky pulled back on the stick. The plane shuttered as it struggled to change direction. The last thing that Lucky could remember was seeing the right wing of the aircraft folding over and crashing into the cockpit that housed him. Then everything went black.

The next thing Lucky remembered was a strange sensation as he floated towards the ground, dangling from under his white parachute that glistened under the desert sun. He could see the smoldering wreckage of his aircraft below him on the desert floor.

When questioned following the crash, Lucky could provide no answers. Nevertheless, when the remains of the aircraft were studied, the answer was evident. When the starboard wing folded and crushed into the canopy, the impact shattered the rear section of the canopy behind the pilot's seat. The hole was barely large enough to accommodate the width of Lucky's shoulders. All who studied the accident were amazed that the unconscious pilot was able to contort himself in a manner that allowed him to squeeze his body, and the bulky parachute, through the jagged Plexiglas hole. It was a very lucky day for Lucky.

Story #34: Nerves of Steel

Being a test pilot in the 1950's was a very dangerous business. Hugh was old school pilot and one of the best. Some test pilots were superstitious and some were not. Some broke the rules for reasons that will never be known. Hugh was one of these.

Hugh's job that winter was to run a test series on a Douglas-made Navy aircraft that was equipped with a counter-rotating propeller ("prop" for short). This innovative design was to give the plane more thrust and more efficiency.

The counter-rotating props had a sound all their own. It was as if the wind gods were being made angry as the powerful single engine propelled the two three-bladed props in two directions at the same time, effectively counteracting the usual effects of torque on the aircraft's fuselage.

Like Lucky, Hugh's routine that day was to conduct a power-on dive. It was against the rules, but Hugh lit up a cigar as the plane struggled for more altitude. Hugh always smoked a cigar when he flew the tests. His superiors wisely looked the other way.

At the appropriate time, Hugh pushed the stick forward, and the large bird pivoted into a vertical dive. As it streaked towards the desert below, Hugh calmly spoke via radio to the tower personnel and the engineers, who were intensely listening in the hanger. At the proper moment, Hugh pulled back on the control lever, but the control surfaces did not respond, and the plane continued on its path towards destiny.

Hugh's voice never wavered as he explained in exquisite detail the things he believed malfunctioned in the control systems. Due to the design of the aircraft, there was no way that Hugh could escape through the canopy without being cut in two by the vertical stabilizer at the rear of the craft.

Tower personnel and hanger engineers watched and listened in stunned horror as Hugh quietly continued his technical explanations as to the causes of failure. His unrelenting descriptions were unabated up until the time the aircraft smashed into the desert floor at over 400 miles per hour.

When the crash site was inspected, Hugh's body was recovered and his teeth were still clenched on his last cigar. It was a sad day at Muroc.

-30-

Hugh's death seemed cruel and unjust; however, his sacrifice and wonderful discipline undoubtedly paved a safer road for future aviators to travel. As our lifestyles have changed, so has our tolerance for risk and sacrifice. From my all-knowing perch, risk and sacrifice must always be worthy goals for humanity or humanity will cease to exist.

Our stay in Mohave ended when the testing was completed on the F84F fighter jet. The trip back to Darke County and our home on the hill seemed to take much longer than the trip that carried us to our western adventure.

When we arrived back in Fort Jefferson, it was clear that nothing much had changed, and this had a comforting effect on me. Dad had chronicled our great adventure in black and white and color photographic slides, and the stories were told to family and friends alike.

Collection #3:

Canvas: Turbulent Times

Setting: 1960-1966. The United States of America, during the 1960's, was a place of searching for both youth and seniors. After the industrious rebuilding of Europe and Japan following World War II, American industry began to decline. At the same time, America was in the process of trying to prevent communist aggression in a little known country called Vietnam. It truly was a time of so-called love, hatred, peace and war, which sounds a lot like every time in all of history.

It was during these years that our grand country began its seductive experimentation into the destruction of the American family. Those who just knew they understood how their fellow Americans should live began to organize into political subgroups where polarization, not unification, was the goal. It was a time when "educators" touted sex *without obligation as the "savior of womanhood" as opposed to "the destructor of the family." Attorneys convicted guns as villains as opposed to convicting villains with guns. Public institutions began teaching our children that lust, greed, avarice, laziness, drunkenness, drug addiction and the commission of murder were diseases instead of human weaknesses to be overcome through knowledge, discipline and honor. Insecure women told strong women that they were weak because they had chosen to raise children with strong values and responsibilities.*

Our government explained to us that our living standards were improving even though economic conditions forced more and more family members to enter the workforce just to maintain status quo. Our government told minorities that they were less intelligent than the majority by lowering college entrance examinations, thus insulting those in the minorities who already had proven the strength, honor and intelligence of their races by finding a way to earn college degrees in many fields of endeavor.

Our government also kept some minorities in mental slavery by telling them that they could not succeed in life without government assistance.

It was a time when the United States of America began to slide into the same death spiral of elitism that has doomed every wealthy culture, in all of recorded history, to decay and eventually vanish into the dust of crushed dreams.

Fort Jefferson had begun to feel the crunch of the changing economics and the community gathering places like Mick Mong and Claude and Summy's general stores succumbed to the pressure. Even in the metropolis of Greenville, family businesses were, one-by-one, supplanted by larger imported conglomerates. Private business ownership and the sense of family, trust, history and knowledge it imparted was being crushed out of existence.

Our federal government had done its job by naming the Soviet Union as our latest "Barbarian on the Border" in order to keep our citizens focused on hatred and fear rather than risk the possibility of sinking into another 1930's-style, self-inflicted economic recession. The nation's most-learned educational institutions were busily cranking out free-spirited wizards who focused their educations on the mass production of such wonder drugs as LSD and crack cocaine so that America's youth could damage their god-given mental facilities and perhaps complete life's journey as dependent vegetables.

It was a time when politicians decided they could prosecute a war better than trained military leaders, and thus broke the spirit of our young fighting force and created an atmosphere where the very people our young soldiers believed they were trying to protect spat upon them. A time where the famous actress, Jane Fonda, thought it was fine to betray her country and fellow citizens by giving notes, passed to her by American prisoners of war, back to the Vietnam guards and torturers.

It was a strange time in American history.

Chapter #8: Finding a Profession

Being raised in Fort Jefferson, Ohio, had many big advantages and a few disadvantages. The small community had a big heart, but it did not have big job opportunities. Therefore, nearly all of its residents were forced to seek employment outside of the village limits. I was no exception. Lord knows that I wanted to be a professional. Heck, I had been professing things, right or wrong, since the day I was born. Becoming a professional seemed like the natural thing to do, but finding a subject upon which to base my professing was another story altogether.

Story #35: The Real McCoy

Greenville High School in the 1960's had traditions, and a sense of excellence and history could be found in these traditions. Like many rural Midwestern communities, Greenville had its share of financial benefactors that paid back the community with numerous monuments. One of these monuments was Memorial Hall, a grand, ornate Victorian theater with a large balcony and two box seats where local dignitaries could show their support and pride.

It was in Memorial Hall where I first really dreamed of being a musician. Of course, my mother played piano and my family did sing together frequently in four-part harmony. I was even given a chance at piano lessons at the age of about nine, but that only lasted a few weeks when my instructor, a wonderful lady, kept making me play a Mozart passage over and over and repeating, "That's not right," after each attempt. Finally, I countered, "I know it's not right, but I like it better my way." That was my last piano lesson. Mom tried to explain to me that it was probably not realistic that I could improve on Mozart.

Brother Bob had played trumpet in the school band and Brother John was still playing cello in the school's orchestra when I arrived in High School. I was singing in the school choirs but playing nothing. During the first half of my sophomore year, I developed Osgood-Schlatter's disease in my left knee and that eliminated my participation in gym class. I hated study halls and one day, while complaining about my predicament at breakfast, Brother John asked, "Why don't you play string bass in the orchestra? The school needs one for next year."

"I don't know how to play bass," I countered.

"You can learn," encouraged John. "Go talk to Mr. Brown."

Mr. Brown

Mr. Brown was a community legend. He was a respected orchestra director and, along with Miss Hill, another community institution, was renowned for musical excellence. Each year the dynamic duo would produce a wonderful spring musical production in Memorial Hall. It had choirs, orchestras, soloists, and vaudeville-type acts. Patrons filled Memorial to capacity for two nights of glorious entertainment.

I mustered my courage, approached Mr. Brown one school day, and boldly stated, "My brother says you need a bass player for next year."

Mr. Brown's bushy white eyebrows bowed downward as he scanned his thoughts. He never said a word, turned and walked away. I followed. Up the stairs into Memorial Hall we went, onward to the second story and then into the orchestra practice room. He shuffled over to a row of great wooden basses, standing like solders in wooden bins, and then pulled a blonde-colored monster from the rack, forced its neck into my hands and said, "Take this home, learn to play it and you can play in my orchestra."

At this point, I must tell a story within a story. How one learns is a most interesting enigma. I used to think that one generally learns from a teacher, but as I grew older, I learned that this is not quite the whole story. One learns through a complex series of interactions among thoughts (theories), people and circumstances. One might think that I learned to play a bass from Mr. Brown. Actually, I learned to play bass through a strange series of events involving my mother, my father, my short-term piano teacher, a jazz musician and Mr. Brown.

As a small child, I would mimic my mother by fingering simple melodies on the large upright piano located on grandma's side of the house. Mom's father had traded a cow for the monstrosity. Later, after being kicked out of piano lessons just because Mozart didn't know how his own music should be played, I continued to plink at the piano in a disorganized fashion. When I reached teenage, a big breakthrough came when I heard music coming from the old piano located on the far side of the house. It was a song that I had heard Mom play many times, but Mom was in the kitchen cooking dinner. "How could this be?" I pondered.

I arose from my Roman relaxation position and sneaked to grandma's side only to find my father sitting in front of the keyboard reading and playing the sheet music located on the piano's music rack.

"I didn't think you played piano?" I stated.

"I don't," said Dad.

"Then how are you reading and playing that music?" I questioned.

"Oh, I just watched your mother play this song several times, and I noticed when she started she struck this key on the piano, so I figured this spot on the music matched that key," he explained.

Just by watching, my father not only had figured out that first note, but also he had correctly guessed all of the musical notations, including rhythms, and was actually playing the song correctly by interpreting this information from the sheet music and applying it to the piano. "How profound," I thought.

I also figured that if Dad could do it, so could I. So, when Mr. Brown gave me the bass with absolutely no instruction other than, "When you can play it, come back and play with the orchestra," I did just that. Brother John told me what notes the bass strings were supposed to be, and I proceeded to figure out how my fingers might achieve the other notes that fell between, below and over the open strings. In addition, I learned where and how those notes would appear on a musical staff.

Within six weeks, I was playing in the high school orchestra, and that same Spring I achieved a seat in the regional orchestra. It was that very same year that a guy named Johnny McCoy came to town to teach music. Mr. McCoy, as I knew him, had been a professional jazz musician before starting his teaching career, and he played his trumpet with some of the best big bands in the country. He also conducted a small group of local professional musicians known as the Johnny McCoy Orchestra that toured a four-state area.

Now I happen to believe in serendipity, and as you may have already guessed, Johnny McCoy was in need of a jazz bass player for his orchestra. My experience with playing a string bass, up until that time, had been in a musical love affair with the likes of Bach, Wagner and Beethoven - not Mozart. This music is very formal by nature and is played with a definite set of rules. Since I was the only kid on the block playing a string bass, I was drafted by Mr. McCoy. However, playing this jazz stuff was hard work and hard learning. The rules were fuzzy and many of them were only inferred, not written on the page. For example, a run of eighth notes in the classical world sounds like a regimented, "Do..do..do..do..do..do..do..do..," while the exact, same notes written in jazz would sound like a more fluid, "Doo.da.doo.da.doo.da.doo.da."

Before long, I found myself touring much of the Midwest with the Johnny McCoy Orchestra, more weekends than not. In the summer months, we might perform for a month or two in a nightclub in Columbus, Ohio.

I was introduced to the world of professional entertainment. Imagine that! A country boy, who spent much of his youth working on farms, hunting or fishing, or just plain loafing, was now a card-carrying professional musician.

I was getting to meet and perform with such stars as the Mills Brothers, a fantastic quartet of black jazz singers. I got to meet such jazz greats as Doc Severnson or my favorite, Clark Terry, better known as "Mumbles." I fell in love with pop singer Barbara McNair of "The Shadow of Your Smile" fame (although she never knew it). I even met the great jazz bandleader Si Zentner of "Up a Lazy River" fame – but that's another story.

It was great. Here I was at 15 years of age, traveling around as a bona fide "professional." I had always wanted to profess something, and I was getting my chance. You have all heard the sordid stories about professional jazz musicians. Now hear the truth. I have never worked as hard and as long as I did as a professional musician. Johnny McCoy, in the music trade lingo, was known as a "hard-nosed son-of-a-bitch." Unbelievably, that is a compliment. Johnny demanded discipline and excellence. Anything less was not tolerated. If you wanted to be a professional, he damn well expected you to perform that way.

Johnny McCoy never asked me to modify the mechanics of my bass playing. He did demand that I improve my musical heart and perfection. He also demanded that I live a straight life and allowed no drinking, smoking, etc., in his presence or on the job site. I honored his wishes and learned much from his dedication, humor and wisdom. I continued to play for the Johnny McCoy Orchestra throughout my high school years and into the summer following my graduation from high school.

It has always been hard for people to believe that a jazz musician could live a "straight-and-narrow" existence, but for me to succeed, it was both mentally and physically imperative that I did so. Strangely enough, regardless of how much I enjoyed my profession as a musician, I was sure that I had not found my life's occupation. I loved music so much that it just didn't seem right getting paid for the performances. My father must have sensed my circumstance and suggested that I look for a more regular profession, which leads me to my next story.

Story #36: A Full-Time Job

From the time I was a very small child, Dad and Mom bundled up the family every fall and then headed north to the deep forests of Michigan. Dad always said he used these trips, "to get my head screwed on straight."

It is hard for city-dwellers and animal rights activists to understand how a person can both love animals and eat them at the same time. I can tell you that it is very possible as I have hunted and harvested my fair share of deer, and there is not an animal on this earth that I respect and honor more. Like many previous North American cultures, I believe that if I am to eat that which God put upon this earth, then I should better understand the taking of the life for my sustenance.

Even during my youthful musical profession, I would cancel work or school activities so I could be available for the annual pilgrimages with family and friends. For years I had fantasized that upon graduation, I would take a great trip of survival to test my manhood. I had planned to take a long canoe trip that would start on Greenville Creek, go down the Little Miami and Great Miami Rivers, then head west on the mighty Ohio River, turn north on the Mississippi River to the old Chicago Canal, then head east through a series of small streams only to end up back in Ohio near my home. A high school chum had agreed to accompany me on the trip, but upon graduation got cold feet and passed on the opportunity. I elected at that time to wait until October, hop on my 15-speed bicycle and head north to my spiritual home in Michigan where I would to live off the land for at least a month.

About now, you are probably wondering what this has to do with a full time job. Well, it was late that summer that Dad suggested that I might want to consider a full-time profession. His suggestion didn't make a lot of sense to me at the time. I was making more money on weekends than most of my friends were making in their full-time jobs. However, I also wanted to grow up and be responsible, although I had no idea what that meant.

Scanning the local newspaper, the Greenville Advocate, I noticed they were advertising for a writer/photographer. My grandfather had been a newspaper owner, my father was an outdoor writer in his spare time and even I had operated a small newspaper known as the "Fort Jefferson News" for a couple of years, starting at the age of nine. I figured that genetics should give me a fighting chance.

I telephoned the newspaper and I was granted an interview with the Editor. His name was Bill, like mine, and I thought this might be of some help. I had never been in a job interview, so this was a very new, unsettling experience.

Bill was a reasonably young man, with a clean-cut appearance. He was articulate and direct.

"So, you want to be a newspaper reporter?" he questioned.

"Yeah, I guess," I replied.

"Did you write for the school newspaper?" he quizzed.

"Nah," I said.

"Were you on the school's Annual staff?" he continued.

"Nah," I said.

"Did you take writing classes?" he asked.

"Nah," I said.

"You did take typing, didn't you?" he quipped.

"Nah," I said.

Following a rather long and drawn-out pause, Bill queried, "What on earth makes you think you can be a writer for this newspaper?"

I had not really prepared for a simple question. Looking at the floor I stated," I did publish a newspaper when I was nine. And, I can take and process black and white photographs."

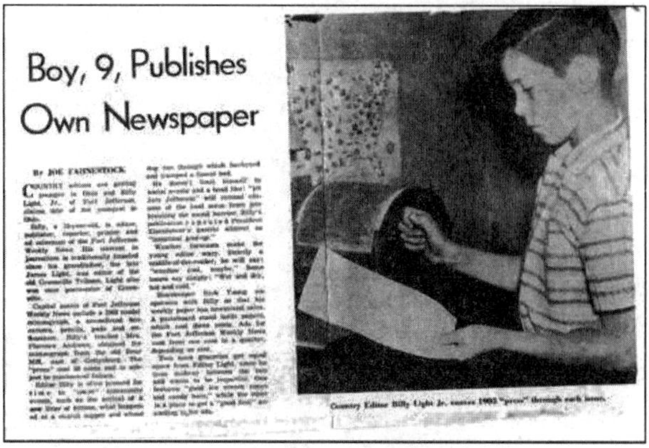

Boy, 9, Publishes Own Newspaper

Bill shook his head in a perplexed fashion and replied, "I have no idea why I'm about to say this, but I'm going to offer you a job." Then, implying that it was most important that I start work in the very near future, he added, "When can you start?"

"Well, it'll have to be in five or six weeks. You see, I'm going to ride my bicycle to northern Michigan and live off the land for a month or so," I stated.

After an even more lengthy silence, Bill looked up and said, "God only knows why I am doing this, but I am going to hire you. Your first assignment is to write a story about your adventure, living off the land in northern Michigan." And, that was that. I had obtained my very first full-time job.

-30-

I have thought about this story over many years and to this day, I have no idea why Bill gave me the opportunity he did. All that I know for sure is that he did and that I began immediate preparation for my northern trek to manhood and to my first full-time job.

Story #37: The Trek North

The day finally arrived to launch my adventure to the north woods. My 15-speed Schwinn road bike had a proven record of accomplishment for distance. I had purchased the bike from one of two Greenville brothers who had decided to circumnavigate the globe on two-wheeled contraptions. One brother successfully completed the journey, but the one from which my bike came was called back early by his draft board to serve in Vietnam. It is funny how a proven record of accomplishment can bolster one's confidence.

As the departure day approached my resolve weakened, but as word of the pending journey spread around the community, there was no chance of a comfortable withdrawal. Moreover, what would happen to my first full-time job? I sure couldn't give up a new job before it started.

My 15-speed bicycle was constructed for racing, not for survival treks. Consequently, I had to fabricate a special holding rack mounted over the rear wheel to hold my travel belongings. When the rack was fully loaded with my goods, the front wheel of the bicycle had to be tied down to prevent it from rising into the air. My total baggage included:

- Two changes of clothing.
- One wool coat.
- A small tool kit.
- A plastic tarpaulin.
- One sleeping bag.
- One dozen arrows.
- One Bear Archery Company 45-pound bow.
- One throwing knife.
- One skinning knife.
- Two pairs of moccasins.
- One pair of tennis shoes.
- One washcloth and one towel.
- One bar of Ivory soap.
- Two sandwiches.
- One bottle of water.
- One plastic cup.
- Two rolls of toilet paper.
- Some waterproof matches.
- One flint and steel.
- $35 cash.

There was not a king on earth that was better off than me as I carefully loaded my bike on a warm and sunny Fall day and then pedaled north on State Route 127. About three miles north of Greenville, I paused for a moment to look back. A thought crossed my mind. It was, "Are you out of your mind?" However, it was too late. I knew I had to continue on my great adventure.

As dusk approached at the end of the first day, I was approaching a small farm located just north of Paulding, Ohio. A large combine was parked in the driveway, and several farmers were busily working on the great machine that had jammed during critical harvesting operations. Sometimes an outside pair of eyes can see that which is not obvious to those in the fray, and minutes after stopping to lend a helping hand, we restored the combine to good working order.

The farm family directed numerous questions toward this strange-looking traveler/repairman who mysteriously dropped in unannounced. They offered me a meal, but I requested that they let me spend the night in the hayloft of their large, white barn. Early the next morning, as I was preparing to leave, I was invited to a fine breakfast, which I gladly accepted. My body restored, I pedaled north under a sunny, cool sky and after only about two miles of travel, I sighted my first deer of the journey. Deer have always held a mystical attraction for me. Their gracious movements and spectacular athleticism generally restores my soul and faith in the higher power that created such artistry.

By the end of day two, I had reached the north side of Jackson, Michigan. I decided to splurge and spend the majority of my $35 on a motel room. My choice turned out to be the Best Motel, owned by Mr. and Mrs. Best, a couple of advanced years. I paid for the room in advance and asked Mr. and Mrs. Best if it would be okay if I disassembled the wheels of my bike in the room, in order to grease the bearings. They consented, with reservation. Later that night there came a knock at my door and when opened, there stood Mrs. Best. "Would you like to talk a bit?" she asked.

I invited Mrs. Best into the cramped room, and she quizzically watched as I worked on my bike. I did my best to answer her numerous questions. A short time later came another knock on the motel room door. It was Mr. Best, who was invited to the party, and the questions and stories continued. It is funny how such gatherings and the resultant stories are stored in the human brain. Even though this evening was a minute snippet in the long thread of my life, I can remember the conversations in vivid detail some 40+ years later.

It was late before the Bests exited my room. They wished me a safe journey and headed for their comfortable house located at the front of the motel. I slept peacefully that night. Before sunrise the next morning, I tied fast my load and pedaled toward the highway. As I passed the Best's home, Mrs. Best was waiting.

"Come on in for breakfast," she said.

"Oh, thanks, but I better be on my way," I declined.

"No, no," she continued. "It's already on the table and Mr. Best is in there waiting for us."

The breakfast was great as was the conversation. I learned more about the Bests and their children. When breakfast was consumed, we said our farewells. As I mounted my bicycle, Mrs. Best handed me a sealed envelope and gave me strict instructions that it was not to be opened until I had left town. I waved goodbye several times, and pedaled away. I can remember being sad about leaving my newfound friends.

The weather rapidly deteriorated as I continued north on Highway 27. It began to rain. Then the temperature dropped and the wind speed rose. The rain turned into a bitter sleet that stung my frozen cheeks, and my hands began to feel numb. I pulled the bike to the side of the road and quickly stretched my plastic tarp over a fence and staked it into place with arrow shafts. Huddling under the tarp, I decided to pass the time by opening the envelope that Mrs. Best had passed to me. Inside was a small card stating, "Good luck and a safe journey. Hope you bag a buck." The card also held a full refund of my motel bill. There is great power in small things. Such an elegant gesture of unsolicited kindness branded a lasting impression on me.

Day 3 carried me to Higgins Lake and on the morning of day four, I stopped at the Bear Archery Company in Grayling. Fred Bear, who founded the company on his superb engineering expertise and love of archery, was a family friend. I had hoped he would be at the factory when I arrived but he was not. The shop foreman gave me a tour of the facilities. Upon completion of the tour, the foreman glanced out the window and noticed my bicycle parked in the snow-covered lot.

"Where did you say you were from?" he quizzed.

"Greenville, Ohio," I responded.

"Where's that?" he asked.

"Just northwest of Dayton about 30 miles," I said.

The foreman had a perplexed look on his face and then continued, "Anyone crazy enough to ride a bicycle 400 miles north in this weather deserves an award. Come with me."

We walked back a long aisle to a small room on the left. When the foreman opened the door, my eyes were greeted with a fantastic sight – thousands of cedar-shaft arrows arranged like toy soldiers in neatly stacked, open cardboard boxes. I was speechless.

"Take any box you like," the foreman smiled.

I felt like a young child turned loose in a candy store as I pawed through the boxes, one after another, looking for the right draw-length, the right spine strength, the right fletch and the right color. After making my selection, the foreman and I said our goodbyes. I left the building and tied my newfound treasure onto to already excessively loaded-down bicycle. Then it was back on the road, with only a half-day jaunt to my goal – Montmorency County and Rush Lake.

I did reach my destination on the fourth day and I did set up camp in the middle of the forest near Rush Lake. There was plenty of time to ponder my four-day, coming-of-age trek and the bonding that occurred along the way with the strangers-turned-friends. It is doubtful that a young man on a bicycle would be greeted in like manner by total strangers in today's cynical 21st century. More likely, police would be called to track the stranger and the archery equipment would be confiscated for fear of a future school massacre. Within two weeks, my body acclimated to the cool October and November temperatures. Most of the time I wore no shirt, and most mornings I bathed in Rush Lake or nearby streams. During the entire adventure, I never caught a cold.

Chapter #9: Northwood Stories

Most people have a special place where the world seems to be in balance. My parents allowed my brothers and me to run free in the forests of Montmorency County, Michigan. Perhaps it was this freedom or perhaps it was the solemn grandeur of the lakes, streams and forest that always made me feel at home. In addition, many of the local residents were rugged individualists who had stories to tell, or they themselves were the stories.

Story #38: The Blacksmith

Living off the land and alone during late fall in the north woods of Michigan can get quite lonely. After about two weeks of eating squirrels and bitter acorns, I decided to seek out some company.

Montmorency County in 1964 was a wooded wonderland of young pine, birch, poplar and oak trees interrupted by numerous lakes and streams. The population of Montmorency County was very small, and my earliest remembrance was that only two paved roads ran through the county – one from south to north and the other from east to west. By 1964, there were three paved roads in the entire county. It was my second home. It was a place where, my father often said, "I can get my head screwed back on straight."

The narrow tires on my 15-speed bike, that had so faithfully carried me to my precious spiritual home, became useless on the two-track sand trails that weaved and wound through the hills and up-ground swamps. So, like my distant cousin Davy Crockett, I was destined to make all my journeys by foot. It was on one of these excursions that I met old Bill Monroe. No, not the country music star of yesteryear. This Bill Monroe was a real character who helped me understand the power of the story.

When I met Bill, he was living in a small log cabin located on a bluff overlooking Rush Lake. Bill was in his mid-70s and sported a full mop of white hair. He was short and wiry, and he had lived through the Great Depression. The year before I met him, Bill and his girlfriend had survived a serious auto accident. His back was broken along with one leg and several ribs. During our time together, he amazed me by riding my bicycle on the sand trail in front of the cabin.

Bill was a storyteller. During the daylight hours, we would cut firewood to feed the cast iron stove that sat in the middle of the small cabin. When the sun disappeared behind the trees, and the thermometer began to fall, we would stoke up the fire, and Bill would tell stories about the people, places and history of Montmorency County until one or the other of us would doze off. The last man standing was relegated to blowing out the solitary kerosene lantern. The pungent fragrance of extinguished lantern, the rich aroma of the wood stove's birch-bark fuel and the snap and crackle of the glowing embers melted the worries away and helped to glue Bill's stories in my mind.

Bill had been a blacksmith for his entire life. He shod horses for the lumbermen that cut the large white pines to build the houses for a rapidly expanding America. He had survived the depression by shoeing horses for State of Michigan road crews and was proud of the fact that he was never out of work.

Most of Bill's stories were only one or two lines long. But, the messages were clear and lasting. For example, one evening Bill suddenly asked, "Do you know Hillman?"

Hillman is a pleasant rural Michigan town located about 20 miles east of the cabin.

"Yes. I know Hillman," I responded.

With a ornery glint in his aged eyes Bill continued, "During the depression there weren't many jobs around here so a lot of guys put their wives to work. Hell, if you could-a put a roof over that town, you-da had the biggest whorehouse in the world," he added.

To this very day, every time I pass through Hillman I envision a huge roof hovering over the town.

It was Bill who first taught me how the best plans of well-meaning politicians usually do not get the desired results.

"Up here during the depression work was hard to come by," he explained. "Most of the guys would start forest fires 'cause the State would pay them a dollar a day to put 'em out. Damn near burned down the whole southern peninsula."

Bill's brief story wasn't exaggerated as much as you might think. Fire destroyed much of Michigan's pristine white pine forests during the Great Depression and many, if not most, of these fires were manmade.

Bill Monroe wasn't the only character in the north woods of Montmorency County, Michigan. His good friend and friend of my family was Ory Mowry. Ory was not so much of a storyteller. He was more of a story maker, and the stories told of him are legion. Meet Ory as the thread of the stories continues.

Story #39: The Story Maker

Ory was a raw-boned old woodsman who wore a black patch over his missing left eye and he never wore shoes. He was the only man I ever saw who could weed a garden with his toes without ever bending over. Consequently, no one thought it odd when he would arrive at the cabin, wading through ankle-deep snow, barefooted. Ory had a standing bet with Atlanta locals and tourists that he could be

blindfolded and taken to any location in Montmorency County, and when unmasked, he could, within five minutes, tell exactly where he was located. He never lost a bet.

Ory was a man of infinite useful knowledge. For example, he once told me, "If you are ever jack-lighting deer at night, only fire one shot, 'cause the game warden can't tell from where the shot was fired with just one noise."

For those non-hunters, jack lighting deer is now an illegal activity where hungry folks used a bright light to illuminate a deer at night in order to get an easy meal or two. The practice was quite common during the Great Depression when Montmorency County had little work and fewer farms. When outlawed by the State, the practice continued in a clandestine fashion. In 1964, one conservation officer explained to me that they did not generally arrest local jack-lighters that they knew were using the food to feed their families.

It was always rumored that Ory was jack lighting deer one night when he saw the bright glitter of a deer's eye in the distance. He took careful aim and fired his one shot. Unfortunately, the glitter was actually the reflection of the chrome grill of the local conservation officer's car.

Ory had a pet black bear that he had raised from a cub. The bear was more like one of Ory's sons, and the two would often run down the hill to splash into Rush Lake for a brisk morning dip.

Ory loved to drink beer and so did his bear. The bear would grasp a bottle between his two paws and down the contents without taking a breath. It was not unusual for Ory to load up the bear in his rusty truck and drive the 10 miles to Atlanta, where he owned a small grocery store.

Many of the town folks, who weren't on a first-name basis with the bear, found the visits unnerving. Unfortunately, complaints were filed and Department of Natural Resource officers were dispatched to tell Ory that he would have to give up his bear. Now, this did not sit well with Ory and by sheer coincidence, the notification came to Ory the same week that the Montmorency County Fair was held in Atlanta. Ory and the bear, both obviously suffering great depression from the sad news, consumed great amounts of beer to drown their sorrows, then both jumped into the truck and headed for the fair. I talked to one of Michigan's conservation officers following the incident and he explained, "To tell you the truth, I don't know who was worse, Ory or the bear." No one was hurt in the encounter, but Ory was forced to part with his black buddy.

When Ory was young and ready to join the labor force, he headed to a nearby local lumber camp to seek employment. He arrived at camp late one evening and was given a job by the camp supervisor, who told Ory to find a place to sleep in the camp bunkhouse. By the time Ory reached the bunkhouse, the veteran lumbermen already were in their beds, so Ory bumped his way down the narrow isle between the bunks. Before reaching a vacant berth, a gnarled hand jutted out from the darkness and stopped Ory in his tracks. Out of the blackness came a deep voice asking, "You got bugs?"

Ory thought for a second and then replied, "Nope."

The voice from the abyss pronounced, "Ya will have!" Then the hand retracted back into the darkness.

The voice from the darkness was right – Ory did get bed bugs that very night.

During one of my family's annual archery deer-hunting trips to Rush Lake, my father had brought along two engineering friends from his workplace. These friends were not experienced woodsmen nor did they know the legendary Ory. At the cabin one evening, Ory arrived to see how everyone was doing. After greeting us and sizing up the newcomers, Ory announced to my father, "Say James, I got a hunger for some chicken. How's about I go into town and grab a couple?"

Ory had a twinkle in his eye as he spoke. Then he looked at one of the strangers and said, "Why don't you ride along with me to keep me company?"

The stranger agreed and the pair hopped into Ory's pickup truck and headed to Atlanta. As Ory turned the truck down a dark alley, he turned off the headlights and continued to drive slowly until he reached a chicken coup located off the left side of the alley. Ory leaped from the truck, opened the coup, grabbed two of the live chickens, then scrambled back to the truck. He stuffed the chickens into the stranger's hands and then ordered, "Hold these!" Then, he crammed the truck into to gear and tore out of the alleyway without turning on his headlights.

The stranger stared silently in total amazement as Ory drove the sand-trailed "back way" out of Atlanta in total darkness. When the truck arrived back at camp, Ory took back the chickens, rung their necks and began plucking the feathers. The bewildered stranger rushed into the cabin where he announced that Ory had just stolen two chickens and that he, most likely, would be arrested as an accomplice to the crime.

It was not until later in the week that the stranger learned that the "stolen chickens" actually were taken from the chicken coop owned by Ory and located behind his small grocery. The birds tasted great.

-30-

It is amazing what fun a group of humans can have when their stations in life are forgotten or ignored. Self-sought or assigned social status can be a great divider of humanity.

Story #40: A Quiet Man

THE QUIET MAN

Ory Mowry had two sons. One son went into the real estate business while his other son, Eldon, helped his father maintain the necklace of small log cottages that graced the east shore of Rush Lake. Eldon was in his mid-60's when I arrived at Rush Lake on my bicycle adventure. He was a quiet, tall, raw-boned man with great strength and patience.

I was amazed by

Eldon's strength and agility for a man of advanced age. On numerous occasions, we would grab two axes and head to the forest to search for fallen trees that could be cut up for firewood. Eldon, over 40 years my senior, played the axe better than some professional musicians play violin. He could strip the side limbs and then cut up three trees into cordwood in the same time it took me to dissect just one.

Eldon seldom spoke more than three or four words at a time. In addition, he hardly ever initiated a conversation. However, he would respond to questions with carefully thought-out and truncated expressions.

A conversation with Eldon would go something like this:

Me: "Think it'll rain today?"

Eldon: "Nope."

Me: "How far do we have to go to get to the dead falls?"

Eldon: "Couple miles."

LONG PAUSE

Me: "I saw two bucks and a doe yesterday."

Eldon: "Did ya?"

Me: "Yes. I nearly got a shot at the one buck, but I could not get an arrow through the thick stuff. I think I may go back tomorrow and still hunt. They might come back there. Of course, there might be a better spot. Maybe where we are going will show some signs. Maybe there will be an old 8-pointer just waitin' for me. What do you think?"

Eldon: "Don't know."

LONG PAUSE

LONGER PAUSE

Me: "Are you hungry?"

Eldon: "Na."

REAL LONG PAUSE
Me: "Are we about there?"
Eldon: "Yup."
BRAKES SQUEEK
DOORS OPEN
AXES GRABBED
CUT WOOD

As you can see, Eldon was a master of concise conversation.

There wasn't much entertainment around Rush Lake, but there was a bar in downtown Atlanta that had a jukebox. When Saturday night came around, Eldon and his wife would hop into their old sedan and head for the "big city." On one particular Saturday night, I was invited to go along, and I felt honored.

We took the north-south paved road into town and had no sooner walked into the bar than Eldon and his wife put a quarter into the music machine and began to dance. Being a professional jazz musician, I had not seen many 60-year-old couples dancing to country music. It was easy to pick them out of the crowd because there wasn't any crowd. Several good-old boys were hunched over the bar, and I was seated at a small round table. That was it.

I watched the graceful and steady couple glide around the floor for hour after hour, pausing only to drink a few beers. Whether or not they talked during the dancing I could not tell, but it was very clear they were communicating in some ancient physical language that I had not yet learned.

It was 1AM Sunday before we left the bar. Both Eldon and his wife, by this time, were unsteady on their feet. As we approached the car, Eldon's wife pushed him aside and shouted, "You're not driving. You're too drunk." From my young *perspective, Eldon's wife seemed more removed from reality than he.*

Eldon obligingly shuffled to the passenger side of the car, and I hopped into the rear seat. It was a journey to remember as we headed north on the "back way" to Rush Lake. This narrow two-track sand trail weaved around numerous pine trees and hardwood stands. The headlights of the sedan would sweep back and forth, occasionally highlighting a grazing deer or a porcupine headed for a nighttime rendezvous. There was not a single word spoken during the entire trip.

How we made it "home" that night is way beyond my comprehension of natural phenomena, but we did and I would not trade the adventure for all the tea in China.

-30-

I have always been a man of many words. Try as I have, a fix or even partial reduction of verbiage has never been forthcoming. Consequently, those who can communicate on an "as needed" basis thoroughly fascinate me.

Eldon remained a close family friend over many years and our different language styles never seemed to matter.

I have been told on numerous occasions that it took great courage for me to head north to my spiritual home in Michigan with $35 and a bicycle. I have learned that courage is usually spawned and supported by knowledge. It is hard to fear that which you love and understand. Thanks to my close-knit family, I was privileged to have spent many hours of my childhood exploring the forests and plains of Montmorency County. Therefore, for me, it seemed quite natural to commune with the wildlife.

It is because I have watched the natural world shrink to dangerous levels during my lifetime that I wish to share some of stories before all understanding of a more simple life is lost in the name of progress.

Story #41: Doctors' Week Out

As the month-long survival expedition continued, my appearance, attitude and strength began to change - significantly. I had grown a mustache and beard, and my hair had grown in a helter-skelter fashion. My skin had been browned by the sun and red blood vessels surfaced on my cheeks.

The constant walking and stalking game gave me added stamina, and I became very tolerant of the cold temperatures. In fact, when the thermometer read 30 degrees or even lower, I would hike about comfortably in my shirtsleeves.

The Michigan soil in Montmorency County is very sandy. On one bright October morning, I was walking a sand trail carrying my bow and wearing no shirt, a pair of blue jeans and knee-high moccasins when I noticed a high-priced automobile approaching me from the opposite direction. When the car pulled along

side of me, it stopped and the driver-side window was rolled down. Seated in the vehicle were two very distinguished looking gentlemen who looked very out of place.

"Good morning," the driver said in a very formal manner. "I see you are an archer. Have you been shooting long?"

I explained that I had been shooting bows and guns since early childhood.

"Do you think you could teach us to shoot bows?" he questioned.

After a brief conversation, I learned that these two dapper-looking gentlemen were physicians out of Detroit, who in their advanced years had decided to go on an adventure and hunt big game in the north woods. Neither had ever ventured into the woods, let alone hunt a deer with a bow and arrow. In fact, they did not even own a bow between them nor did they know where to get one.

I agreed to give it a shot and told them that I would meet them in front of Mowry's cabin on Rush Lake the next morning. When I awakened early the next day, the doctors were waiting. I fixed breakfast on the cabin wood stove and we drafted a plan. Of course, there were stories to tell along the way. They seemed fascinated when I told them that I had been living mostly on squirrels and acorns.

"I thought acorns were poisonous?" one questioned.

You would have thought a doctor would have known about such things, but he didn't. I explained that they were a bit bitter, but the acorns from the white oaks tasted much better than those from red oaks.

When I told them that I had been catching squirrels by hand, they looked at me in disbelief again. I explained that shooting at squirrels with arrows was a risk, because a miss could mean a missing arrow and I had begun the journey with only one dozen. Moreover, I surely wasn't going to lose one of those beautiful shafts given to me by the Bear Archery foreman by shooting at some dumb squirrel.

Now you may be thinking that this is a tall tale, but it is not. You see, Michigan black squirrels are a strange breed. When they are binge feeding in the fall of the year, they will do just about anything to keep from climbing high into a tree. During my first two solitary weeks in the woods, I had plenty of time to observe the behaviors of these squirrels. I learned that when frightened, squirrels run on the ground as fast as they can, and they will run on a line that keeps tree trunks between them and their adversary. I also learned that squirrels are quick, but not fast runners.

However, let's get back to the doctors.

"What? You say you want to know how to catch a live black squirrel with your bare hands. Okay, okay.....I'll get back to the doctors in a minute or two."

Warning: Mothers, you may wish to keep this information away from your young sons, as the following could be hazardous to their health. Fathers, you may wish to encourage your sons in such endeavors as it quickens their reflexes and gives them a great respect for the teeth of squirrels. Besides, it's fun to watch.

How to catch a squirrel:

1. Find a spot in the woods where the black squirrels congregate to feed on acorns and such.
2. Learn the time of day and the type of weather they prefer.
3. Position yourself in the feeding area before daylight and sit absolutely still until the sun rises and the squirrels begin to feed.
4. Pick out a larger, tastier looking squirrel of advanced years. (Forget about how an old squirrel might taste.)
5. Jump to your feet and scream at the top of your lungs and run towards the target squirrel as fast as you can, being careful never to take your eyes off the squirrel.
6. Make as much noise as you can as you crash through the forest. If the squirrel heads for a tree, change direction to the left or right slightly, so you can better see the squirrel when it tries to position trees between you and its planned path.
7. Keep chasing until the squirrel tires and eventually runs up the opposite side of a tree from you.
8. Here is the secret: When a black squirrel runs up the opposite side of the tree, he will only go about five or six feet above the ground.
9. Very, very quietly approach the tree on your same direction of travel, keeping the tree between you and the squirrel.

10. Listen carefully and you will hear the squirrel's claws scratching the bark of the tree as he squirms to position himself for a quick escape. Use your ears to imagine the height of the squirrel's position on the opposite side of the tree.
11. With as much quickness as you can muster, reach around the tree with both arms and tightly grab the squirrel with both hands.
12. For God's sake, squeeze tight, or you will find out exactly how sharp a Michigan black squirrel's teeth are.

Now let's get back to the doctors.

As the doctors and I worked our way through stacks of Bill Monroe's Famo pancakes and slurped some boiled coffee, I did manage to come with a plan for the day.

"What? You say you never drank boiled coffee. Okay, okay. I will give you the recipe.

How to Boil Coffee:

1. Find a large, I mean really large, enamel coffee pot (about 1-1/2 gallons).
2. Dump in about one-half pound of coffee. (Any kind will work. If it smells stale, it is even better.)
3. Fill the pot with water.

(Preferably, use well water from a shallow well.)

4. Place the pot on a wood-burning stovetop or an open fire and bring the water to a full boil.
5. Move pot to a cooler location on the stove or open fire and allow simmering at a low boil for about an hour.
6. Remove the pot from the stove and place in a still position in a camp sink or on the ground.
7. Gently pour cold water over the outside of the pot for about 15 seconds. (This causes the grounds to settle.)
8. Wait until the coffee drops to drinking temperature and then carefully pour the coffee into tin mugs, being careful not to stir up the grounds. (Do not burn your hands on the mugs.)
9. Re-heat pot as needed, but do not bring to a full boil.
10. **WARNING:** Drinking boiled coffee at camp will bring on vivid dreams like those that you have never had before. If you have a heart arrhythmia, do not take the chance, despite the great dreams.

Now, where were those doctors? Oh yes, just finishing breakfast and ready to begin studies in Shooting Bows #101.

The doctors loaded me up in the back seat of their high-priced automobile and we headed to Atlanta where they purchased two bales of straw, a brightly colored circular archery target, two bows, two dozen fine cedar arrows, finger tabs, arm guards and two quivers to hold the arrows. Then it was back to camp.

As you might expect from two formally trained physicians, they wished to see an example of my shooting skills before accepting me as their instructor. I have to admit I did not look much like a certified teacher, but I had shot moveable target demonstration archery for Bear Archery Company, and I already had learned how to profess as a professional musician. What more could they want?

We set one bale of straw on top of another, and then positioned the brightly colored, circular target on the center of the bales. I strung my bow and was just about to begin the shooting exhibition when one of the doctors asked, "How far can a bow like that shoot?"

"I'll show you," I said. Then I paced off about 180 yards, turned around, set an arrow on the string, pulled to full draw, and then aimed skyward at an angle to achieve maximum range. The object here was to go for distance in order to fulfill the doctor's request – not hit the target.

When the arrow was released, it made a grand arc towards the target. I had hoped the shaft would land somewhere in the general direction of the straw bales so that I would not have to spend a great amount of time searching for it. However, as if guided by a modern infrared missile guidance system, the arrow honed in on the circular target and punched through the middle of the bright red circle.

The doctors looked astonished as I casually walked the 180 yards back to the target, gently removed the arrow from the exact center of the red ring and placed the shaft back into my quiver.

"Can you do that every time?" one of the doctors queried.

"No problem. Every time," I responded. I never shot another arrow that day, but training went well with my enthusiastic students who, by now, just knew they were studying with a Master.

I am quite sure the two Detroit physicians had a superb time during their great adventure, and I am just as certain that stories of the survivalist, squirrel-catching, expert archer still are told in the Detroit area to this very day. The doctors never shot, or for that matter, never shot at a deer or any other animal that week, but it was clear that they had learned why the Northwood's call is so clear and alluring.

Story #42: Hi Duke

As mentioned in earlier stories, my family was very close, biologically at least. You might say we were the original "All in the Family."

It was always tough to be separated from family and my trek to northern woods was no exception. However, family was to arrive during the last week of my journey, and the anticipation of their arrival was great.

It was uncertain as to when my parents, brothers, sister, cousins and friends would arrive, so I spent the morning woods walking. By the time I had hiked to the cabin on Rush Lake, some of the family already had arrived, unloaded their baggage, tied up the dogs and left for town to purchase supplies. As I walked along the familiar, swamp scent-laden lane to the cabin, I saw my Uncle Dick's (the veterinarian) dog "Duke" tied on a long rope to a tree just outside the cabin. It was the first familiar face I had seen in four weeks.

As I approached Duke, I kneeled down and commanded, "Come here Duke." Duke immediately bared his teeth, issued a deep growl and charged. I leaped backwards and Duke shuttered to a stop when he reached the end of his rope.

I could not believe it. Duke was a large gray Weimaraner with friendly, pale green eyes. He was normally very good-natured and was never known to attack. Weimaraners originally were bred to fight wild boars and bear in Germany. They are powerful, intelligent dogs with keen noses. You do not want a Weimaraner mad at you for any reason.

I figured I must have acquired a bad odor or my appearance had changed so much that Duke didn't recognize me. I spent about 20 minutes trying to rebuild an apparent lost relationship, but Duke would have nothing to do with me. In fact, he would move backwards to put slack in his rope and encourage me to approach so that he could attack. I just had never seen Duke act this way before.

A vehicle approached from the end of the driveway, and as it came into focus, there was my uncle and family returning from their shopping trip. There was the usual re-acquaintance ritual of hugs and handshakes, then we all carried groceries into the cabin and began telling – you guessed it – stories.

When there was a pause in the reunion, I looked at Uncle Dick and asked, "What's wrong with Duke? He 'bout took my leg off. He has no idea who I am."

There was a brief pause, then a smile bloomed on Dick's face, and then he broke out into uncontrollable laughter.

"Duke! Duke!" he laughed. "That's not Duke, that's Gerhard. I just bought him a few weeks ago."

-30-

I find it strange how humor tends to spring from unpredictable and indefinable events - things that have neither shape nor form. It is recognized from some perspectives but not from others. It took me some seconds to appreciate fully the perspective that brought my uncle to his knees in laughter. I could have been killed or maimed, but I had not been. Surviving is truly a "funny" thing. It has been said that those pioneers who survived the perilous journeys west in covered wagons had wonderful senses of humor and those who died along the way did not. Psychologists argue whether it was the surviving pioneers' senses of humor that carried them over the mountains or whether they gained the sense of humor after the survival. There is no question in my mind that one must laugh in the face of danger – however painful that danger might be.

As you may have already guessed, many of the stories in this book do not necessarily appear in chronological order. That is just the way it is with stories. There always is some thread that sews the stories together; however, they might not be together at the same time. Such is the case with the next chapter.

Chapter #10: Legends of the North

Montmorency Country, Michigan was a special place for not only my family but also the many friends that joined us in our numerous pilgrimages to this land of promise that time seemed to have forgotten.

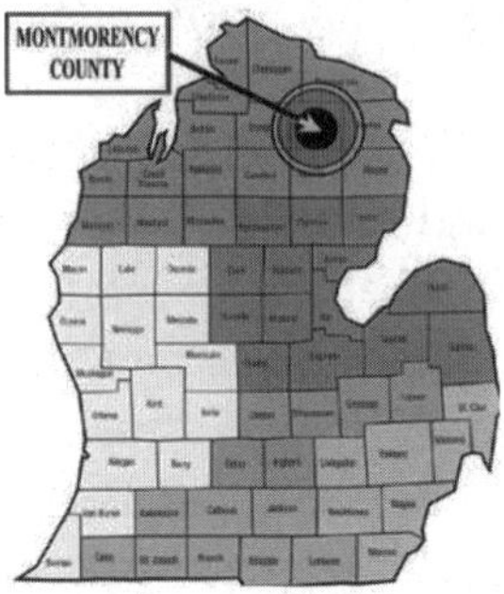

It really is hard to put into words the emotions evoked by Montmorency County. While the world, still reeling from world conflict, seemed to be changing at an exponential rate during the 1960's and 1970's, Montmorency County appeared to be stuck in a very welcomed time warp. However, the forests of Montmorency did not harbor stands of mature Michigan white and red pines, giant red and white oaks and large-girth birch. The old forests had disappeared earlier in the 20th century by means of logging or forest fires. In the 60's and 70's, the Montmorency trees and fauna were new and refreshing. This rebirth sparked a huge increase in wildlife, especially the white-tailed deer. Other critters that made the county their home were black bears, beavers, roughed grouse, turkeys, elk, snowshoe rabbits, prairie chickens, raccoons, porcupines, fox and black squirrels, timber doodles (woodcocks), red fox, chipmunks, snapping turtles, leatherbacks and so forth.

Since most of my family boasted generations of hunters and anglers, Montmorency County seemed to be the place that Norsemen called Valhalla. It was a place where you could still experience a universe of profound silence, especially when napping in an up-ground swamp on a foggy fall morning. It was somewhere that the crisp snap of a single twig could cause your mind to imagine the approach of a giant black bear. Perhaps a whitetail buck would silently materialize in a bright sliver of sunlight, then, in a split second, magically disappear without a sound.

The Light family treks to our treasured open space came in two forms – fall and summer. The autumn visits were usually one or two-week adventures with family and friends that primarily focused around the hunting of whitetail deer, grouse and rabbits, with a limited emphasis on fishing for northern pike or largemouth bass. The summer visits were more for family only and consisted of fishing, swimming and exploring new territories. The stories formed, exaggerated and oft repeated during these journeys are legion. Only but a few are listed below.

Story #43: Out of Control

As I arose one summer morning, the sky was crystal blue and Rush Lake was so still that the surface of the water reflected the image of the colorful forest on the far shore in perfect replication. I was the late riser that morning and found myself alone in the log cabin, except for the company of two large Weimaraners. It was so nice out that I decided to load my fishing gear into one of the old wooden boats beached on the sand in front of the cabin, and row out to the channel that ran the length of Rush Lake, from the south inlet to the Sportsmen's Dam at the north end.

I had not been fishing long when I heard the faint sound of an outboard motor approaching. As the small green vessel neared, I could see that it was my brother John at the helm. I assumed he was heading my way to join in the fishing expedition for perch, bluegill and hammer handle pike. However, I assumed wrong.

As the gap between the two boats decreased, I could make out an evil glint emanating from John's eyes. It was the same kind of look you see in the eyes of a wolf, just before it pounces on its unsuspecting meal.

As the bow of John's high-velocity missile got dangerously close to my aged craft, he swung the tiller hard right. The bow wake crashed into the side of my boat, throwing me off balance and nearly hurling me into the chilly water. Repeatedly John took aim, charged and then veered, at the last possible second. Each time I was thrown about my dingy as it tossed to and fro. During one near miss, I noticed his evil glint had changed to a broad smile, but there still was a tint of evil apparent.

It seemed like the buzzing continued for hours, and I was not catching many fish. Finally, without a word, John headed back towards shore and the safety of the cabin. As the outboard engine noise faded in the distance, I felt a brief sense of relief, followed by an increasing need for revenge.

Now I fully understood the Bible passage, "Vengeance is mine, sayeth the Lord," but I guessed that "re-venging" seemed like an activity in which I might legally participate since it most likely happened after the "venging."

It was two days later that I happened to notice one of the wooden rowboats missing from its mooring. Also absent was Brother John. Putting one and one together told me that the two were possibly sitting together in the middle of the peaceful lake – a peace that I was determined to break.

The only motor-powered boat on the lake was another wooden rowboat owned by Ory Mowry and powered by a new Elgin outboard engine that belonged to my Uncle Dick, the veterinarian. Since Uncle Dick was not present at the time of my revelation, you can see that I had no choice but to borrow the boat and motor without asking permission. Opportunities like this seldom happen during a lifetime. Young folks seem to have a natural understanding of this.

I leapt into the boat, dug one foot into the sand to push the craft off shore, clambered to the rear seat, grabbed the starter rope on the outboard engine, and gave her a yank. Two pulls later, the motor sprang to life and off we went, at full throttle, with my sights set directly on John's helpless craft.

It did not take long before John noticed the forthcoming attack. Zoooom.....Zoooom........Zoooom. Like a swooping hawk, I intimidated the prey. John's boat tossed and rocked as the waves slammed against it sides. I was in heaven.

When one is taking revenge, it is especially important that the revenge be more intense than the original offense that was cast upon the "revenger." So, with great gusto, I continued the assault, yanking the motor control arm from one side to the other, causing the boat to lurch back and forth in a jerky manner. Abruptly, without any warning, it felt as if I had a tiger by the tail. It took all of my strength to hold onto the control arm as the motor had ripped half of the boat's transom away and the motor was screaming as it bobbed and weaved and twisted and splashed. Suddenly, my grip failed. The motor made one

last scream before it disappeared under the churning water. The eerie silence that followed is something I will never forget.

If you are not mechanically inclined, I will tell you that it is not a good thing for an outboard engine to be running at full throttle when it sinks to the bottom of a lake. It tends to convert normally straight push rods that connect the pistons to the crankshaft, into S-shaped pieces of scrap metal.

Simultaneously, it struck John and me that a damaged engine might be fixed, but an engine residing on the bottom of Rush Lake was no good to anyone – especially Uncle Dick. It never ceases to amaze me how bright we were as young men. Luckily for us, Rush Lake's water in the fall was extremely clear. When the foam of my assault had dissipated, we could see the engine lying about 15 feet below our perch on the surface. By tying two anchor ropes together, we were able to row upwind, sink the ropes, then drift over the wreck site, attempting to snag the motor. Eventually the rope hooked onto the engine's sediment bulb, and we carefully hauled it to the surface.

Admitting to destroying your uncle's new outboard engine is no easy task. I do not think he was very happy about the incident, but I don't know for sure for I never looked up to read the expression on his face while I admitted the crime.

-30-

People who do not believe in miracles are beyond my understanding. How my brothers and I survived childhood and even young adulthood is, in my opinion, clear proof that there is a God, or at the very least, guardian angels.

Story #44: What Do You See?

Newcomers to the spacious woods of Montmorency County, Michigan, can become disoriented in record time. Even those newcomers who purport to be brave and wise woodsmen can experience lapses of directional orientation from time to time. It has occurred to me that throughout all of recorded history, many of the great sayings of wisdom have stemmed from great explorers who became lost.

It has been said that one of America's most respected mountain men was asked, "Have you ever been lost?"

With little, if any, hesitation he replied, "Hell no! I ain't never been lost, but I've been powerfully confused for a month or two."

My cousin John and his friend Louie had joined our hunting group one year, and we pitched a camp of tents and such on the north end of Jackson Lake, located a few miles south of Rush Lake. A variety of terrain surrounded Jackson Lake, including thick swamp ground.

Even though there was plenty of deer sign around the north side of the lake, Cousin John and Louie decided a successful future could better be found on the south side. Early one afternoon the intrepid duo was floated to the south end by boat and dropped off, alone, in their happy hunting ground.

As evening turned to twilight, all of the hunting party congregated back at camp – all except Cousin John and Louie. As twilight turned to total darkness, our non-lost contingency began to get concerned about their missing comrades.

Several hours after dark, the barking of the camp dogs was interrupted by the crunching of sticks and leaves as the two weary hunters dragged their bodies into the camp lunch tent and parked.

"Where have you guys been?" someone groaned.

"We weren't sure where we were," offered Louie.

"Did you use your compass?" Uncle Dick injected.

"We didn't trust them," came Louie's response. Then he added, "John climbed to the top of a large tree once. I yelled up and asked, 'What do you see?' and John hollered back, 'More trees!'"

There was a lot of laughter in camp that night.

-30-

It turned out that cousin John and Louie had used the barking of the camp dogs to guide them back to camp. If you think I am poking fun at John and Louie, you would be mistaken. In fact, I can't think of anyone who attended our annual adventures that wasn't "powerfully confused for a month or two," at one time or another.

"The grass is always greener on the other side of the hill." I was taught not to believe this lesson early in life, but as I look back on the journey, it seems to me that I, and my family teachers, still believe that some ancient law supports a truth in the axiom. I came to this conclusion while on numerous hunting trips with family and friends. Regardless of ample game sign around our camps, generally we would spend hour after hour scouting many miles away from home base. Driving the sand trails by car or truck allowed us to find fresh tracks that deer left behind on the roadway. For hours on end, the stories were told and retold during these explorations.

Story #45: The Twilight Zone

It was a dark and brisk morning as Brother John, his wife Annie, Uncle Dick and I prepared for a morning of scouting in the "North Country." The North Country was not defined by any map, and yet all of our hunting partners knew its boundaries. It was the large area of state-owned land located north of the "Upper Race Track" (not to be confused with the "Lower Race Track"), and it extended north all the way to Onaway. Now that I think of it, the "Upper Race Track" was not marked on any map either; however, it was located several miles north of the "Lower Race Track." The Lower Race Track was a segment of county road #628 that eventually looped back into the only paved road in Montmorency County.

The North Country was a mystical place where a myriad of two-track sand fire trails wound their way through numerous new growths of pine trees that were planted after the area was destroyed by forest fires. Some of the trails were arranged in neat grids while others started and stopped without warning. No matter which way we would drive, it always seemed that we found a path over which we had never traveled. We expected nothing different as we drove out of camp that fateful morning.

As we headed north, Uncle Dick began telling of an event that occurred when he, my father and our favorite Hungarian bowyer, George LaPois, had taken a similar exploratory expedition several years prior.

Uncle Dick explained that the trio was riding in Dick's station wagon when the deeply rutted sand two-track trail headed skyward. Dick gunned the engine of the car, but about halfway up the steep grade, the tires began to spin and the car came to an abrupt halt. Dick backed the car down the grade and kept going backward until it reached a point where it could get a faster running start. Off they went and the car bounced over the previous stopping point and shuttered its way towards the precipice. Again, it came to a halt, far short of the mark.

"Give her another try," Dad and George encouraged, so it was back down the hill. This time Dick floor-boarded the accelerator pedal and the wagon rocketed up the slope at an alarming pace. The crest of the mini mountain looked obtainable, but the vehicle ground to a halt for the third time, just a few feet from the top.

"Let's take a look at the other side while we're up here," Dad advised.

The trio walked up the final 10 feet to the peak. They stood in stunned silence when they found that the trail ended in a straight down, 100-foot-drop cliff.

We all laughed at Uncle Dick's story as our car left the Upper Race Track and ventured into the North Country. The sun had risen and its rays sparkled off the heavy frost. We occasionally stopped to check out various sets of game tracks that occasionally crossed the trails.

After several hours of driving or riding, conversations tend to peter out and such was the case when someone broke the silence and quietly asked with perplexity, "Does this stretch of woods look real familiar?"

I knew it looked real familiar to me, but none of us could put our finger on why it looked so familiar.

We continued driving for another half hour when the scenery began to look even more recognizable. It was as if we were traveling the same road over and over, but that was not possible because we never made any turns.

John said, "Stop the car!" and Uncle Dick obliged. John hopped from the car, took his skinning knife to cut off a small pine branch from a nearby tree, and then stuck the branch into the trail beside the car. When John returned to the car, we continued our journey. After another half hour, a very familiar pine branch became visible through the front windshield. It was at about this time that I expected Rod Sirling or Allen Funt to walk out of the woods. Neither did.

From all points of view, we had just achieved the impossible and it was not a comforting feeling. We made one more trip into the twilight zone, but again we found ourselves back at the pine branch and we had made no turns and no intersecting roads were seen. I remember asking Uncle Dick if I was awake or if I was dreaming. I think he had been about to ask me the same question.

Stopping one last time at the pine branch marker, Dick decided that I should position myself on the car roof and watch for sign of anything as we bravely drove off again to an uncertain future. Some 10 minutes into this trek, I noticed some grass that had been broken down on a slight hillside at the edge of the trail.

"Stop!" I shouted, then nearly slid off the roof as Dick stood on the brakes,

There it was. A little-traveled, grass-covered, two-track sand trail approached our location on an oblique angle, and then dropped over a slight hill to merge with our trail of no end. With a sigh of relief, Dick turned the car onto the hidden path, and we headed back to camp with a new story.

-30-

Following our brief encounter with the twilight zone, we searched our maps for evidence of the trail with no end. It was not there, which made our story somewhat unbelievable to our fellow hunters. I'm happy to report that current maps of Montmorency County do show a large oval trail located in the middle of our North Country. It has always been surprising to me that no tourists' skeletons have been found on the odd trail.

Unusual events seemed quite normal in Montmorency County. Sometimes the lure of the north woods could even change a person's normal disposition, and one time it did just this to George Lapois.

George Lapois was Hungarian born and a long-term friend of my father. He was short in stature but stout in strength. The gifted bowyer had a keen sense of humor, and his laugh was contagious. The sport of archery drew Dad and George together, and the annual trips to Montmorency County helped to bond George and his family to our extended family tree.

Story #46: Bear Facts

Sometimes things happen when you least expect them. For example, how many times have you thought about someone you have not thought about in a long time, then he suddenly pulls into your driveway or the phone rings and there he is. Or, perhaps you have a deep, hidden fear and for some inexplicable reason, destiny seems to repeatedly force you into facing this fear.

For whatever reason, George Lapois seemed to be cursed by the second example. George had a life-long fear of bears, so deer hunting with bow and arrows where bears are not that uncommon seemed to tempt fate.

George and his hunting partner, Roy Brandes, decided to go on ground stands one sunny October afternoon in the hopes that a whitetail buck might blindly stumble in front of them. The mottled, golden poplar leaves rattled around George and Roy as they sat motionless at the base of their stand trees and they imagined what stories they might tell after bagging their quarry.

Any honest hunter will tell you that sitting at the base of a tree for several hours can test your patience. George had prepared for the anticipated boredom and began unpacking two peanut butter and onion sandwiches, a deer camp staple. Suddenly, there was a rustle to George's left. George deftly seated an arrow on the string of his sinew-backed, Osage orange bow. However, it wasn't a deer that sprang into view; rather a small, chubby black bear cub rolled into the clearing that lay in front of George. George became intrigued as the cub played in its private playground. George laid his bow and arrow aside and began munching on the sandwich. Then he thought, "Roy ought to see this." George abandoned his sandwich, laying it beside its mate on the wax paper wrapper. Then he quietly arose and sneaked back into the woods to find Roy.

Roy was seated about 200 yards away, and when George arrived at Roy's stand, he excitedly explained what had happened and then encouraged Roy to accompany him back to the clearing so that Roy could share in the wonderment. Roy agreed, and the duo retraced George's path. As the two men neared the destination, they went into stealth mode and silently approached the edge of the clearing, then knelt down to see under the pine boughs. Their keen eyes scanned the opening in the forest, but no bear cub was to be seen or heard.

George and Roy headed to George's tree and while lamenting their misfortune, both suddenly froze in stunned silence. There before their eyes appeared an empty wax paper wrapper and two giant black bear tracks in the sand beside the waxed paper. Momma bear had been

watching George as he was watching her cub play in the clearing. With the hair on the back of their necks, standing straight up, George and Roy quickly and quietly picked up their gear and returned to camp.

-30-

Encounters in forests are often unexpected and generally are answered with unplanned and non-logical responses. Such was the case with our next story.

Story #47: A Change of Mind

Food was a focus of attention in hunting camps, and usually it was in short supply. Consequently, about twice a week, a trip was made to the grocery in Atlanta. Two common routes were used to get to Atlanta from Rush Lake. One way was to take the sand trail that led from Rush Lake to #624 (a larger sand trail) that led to #33, the only paved road that ran north of Atlanta. This route took the least amount of time but was not preferred. The favored trail was the "back way" which involved a series of two-track sand trails. This route was favored because deer occasionally were spotted during the journey.

Provisions were running low, so Dad, Uncle Dick, George and Roy loaded up Dick's station wagon and headed to town - going the back way. As the car passed through a valley covered with hardwoods, a large black bear rumbled across the road, causing Dick to apply the brakes. In the excitement of the moment, all four men bailed out of the car, quickly pulled their bows from their cases, grabbed a few arrows, and then began running up the steep hillside in pursuit of the bear.

The foursome was about halfway up the hill when reality began to cross George's mind. In a loud and clear voice George articulated his inner revelation as he shouted, "What in the Hell am I doing chasing a bear?" He immediately reversed his direction, ran down the hill, jumped into the car and shut all of the doors.

-30-

The story of George's reaction to the great bear hunt was told repeatedly in camp that year and for many years to come. No bear ever was bagged, but no one seemed to care. Laughing with, and not at, each other seems to go a long way in fostering acceptance of each other.

Sometimes human beings suffer from an exaggerated sense of pride. It is my opinion that this pride has spawned many of history's superstitions. Our next story will reveal a real-life example of the birth of a superstition.

Story #48: The Whammy

While relaxing one day during my bicycle episode of survival, I found an 18-inch section of Michigan oak heartwood that looked just right for carving. I had never carved anything before, but I did have some knives and I had all my fingers. It seemed to me that this carving stuff could not be that difficult because I had heard they did a lot of whittling in Kentucky. Besides, I had plenty of free time.

It's funny what your hands will do when your mind is at idle. With no real thought, my hands guided the sharp knife-edge about the wood - chopping here, carving there and scraping up, down. It did not take long before one end of the cylinder began to take form. What appeared looked like the head of some ancient Polynesian god, except the god's head seemed to be topped with a Mohawk Indian haircut. The rugged face sported pursed lips and beady eyes that seemed to convey a deep sense of dark wisdom and frustration. The god's neck was three times longer than its head and this neck had a sinewy texture. The entire work of primitive art seemed mysterious, so I named it the "Whammy" in honor of the L'il Abner cartoon series.

The next year I drove my old gray Volkswagen to Rush Lake and moved into the communal cabin. The Whammy moved in with me along with family and my favorite hunting buddy, Fred Falknor. One never knows for sure what attracts and bonds friends together. Some say that opposites attract. I never felt like an opposite to Fred. I felt more like a brother even though Fred was closer to my mother's age than mine was. I could write an entire book called "The True adventures of Fred & Bill," but nobody would believe a word of it.

Fred Falknor
My best friend

Fred admired the Whammy. I explained to him that I was sure it had supernatural powers and that I believed it might be able to bewitch deer into standing still while we shot arrows at them. We decided to carry the Whammy in my Volkswagen during the next morning hunt.

My gray Volkswagen was not in good condition and had a habit of not starting by battery. In such cases, it usually took at least two brothers and a friend to push the vehicle down a sand trail until it reached a speed sufficient to crank the engine. Regardless, we warmed up the engine the next morning, and then loaded our gear and the Whammy.

We had not seen much game that morning so we ventured into the forbidden zones of the North Country near Rainy River Dam Road. Actually, we normally called it "Rainy River – Damn Road" because the trails in the area were unusually rough. I was being very careful not to kill the engine of the VW for fear that we would be stuck in the area for life.

The sun was shining bright as we drove through an expansive clearing that was dotted with piles of brush created by recent timbering activities. All of a sudden, a bevy of roughed grouse ran across the trail ahead of us. I stopped the VW, pulled my double-barrel shotgun from its case, chambered two 12-gauge shells with #7½ shot, closed the chamber and then walked the short distance to the brush pile. Fred walked to my side, serving as a makeshift birddog. Much to our chagrin, no birds flushed from the pile or from the surrounding land.

Fred and I must have spent 15 minutes stomping around the meadow trying to locate the vanished birds. How an entire flock of grouse can disappear in open terrain has always been a mystery to me. As we ambled back to the car, Fred said he was tired of riding and wished to drive for a while. I tried to discourage him and explained that if he accidentally killed the engine, we might be stuck there for days. He didn't care and insisted that he drive.

We had not traveled over 200 yards when we rounded a small curve and there, not more than 25 yards from Fred's side of our car was a deer broadside and standing in wide-open terrain. Those of you non-hunters should understand that the deer in Montmorency County are very used to outsmarting hunters. If humans and whitetail deer were to play a football game, I'm sure the score would end up as Deer 1,657, Humans 3. I tell you this so that you will understand that Fred and I fully expected the deer to bolt and disappear moments after Fred stopped the VW. As Fred slowed the car, I reached for the Whammy and handed it to Fred.

"Aim this thing at the deer," I ordered.

Fred aimed the Whammy at the deer while I tried to get out of the car, unpack my bow from its case, string the bow, reach in for an arrow, place the arrow on the string, sneak to the back of the VW, pull back the bow and then let an arrow fly towards the deer. Nothing to it!

Anyone in his right mind, including me, would know the sequence described above could not happen. However, when Fred aimed the Whammy towards the deer, the animal seemed to be mesmerized as it stared intently at the unusual looking wooden god. On the other hand, it could have been staring at Fred. Whatever the case, time seemed to stand still as I accomplished the required sequence of events and let the arrow fly. The arrow, with surgical precision, hit its mark; the deer ran a few yards and then collapsed. Fred immediately turned off the ignition of the car.

There we sat – Fred, a dead deer, the Whammy and me in the middle of nowhere with a vehicle that would not start unless four strong human bodies could push it.

Things could have been worse. I might have shot Fred. If nothing else, we would have food to eat if we were stranded for a lengthy period of time. After cleaning the deer and tying it on the VW, I told Fred to aim the Whammy at the VW while I tried to start it. As if possessed, the starter motor functioned perfectly and the VW roared to life. Another miracle had been witnessed. Fred shook his head and hopped in.

"Should we even mention this in camp?" Fred asked as we proceeded down the trail.

"I donno," I answered.

That night, after the evening feast, the hunting clan began its usual ritual euchre card game around the large circular table. Played by teams of twos, these card games were quite competitive. No money exchanged hands, but bragging rights were important. This particular night it was Uncle Dick and my Brother Bob who wanted to challenge a less experienced team consisting of Fred and me. We agreed to the challenge.

Please understand that this card game was played shortly after Fred and I relived our deer story, including the part about the power of the Whammy. Fred and I almost got laughed out of camp. Also, understand that teams must win 10 hands to win one game in euchre.

As the two teams addressed the table, I made sure that I placed the Whammy conspicuously on the table and aimed its beady eyes directly at my older Brother Bob. No words were spoken as the cards were shuffled and dealt.

Fred and I won several hands and even won the first game. This was unusual in itself, but what happened next was beyond statistical probability. Fred and I continued to win hand after hand and game after game. After about six wins, my Brother Bob casually reached over, grabbed the Whammy and then set it on the floor.

I quickly reached down, lifted the Whammy off the floor, replaced it on the table, and aimed it directly at my Brother Bob.

"Get that damn thing off the table," a grumpy Bob grumbled. "It doesn't belong there."

"It looks okay to me," Fred commented.

Had I said those words, Bob most likely would have argued. For some reason, he said not a word.

The card games continued and the Fred-Bill team continued to win hand after hand and game after game. The hour was getting late, so after 13 straight game wins, all participants agreed to quit – some happier than others.

Later in life, I became interested in analytical statistics. I have never really been a superstitious person, but even I have to admit that the odds of winning 13 straight euchre games is a near impossibility, regardless of the skill of the teams. As Grandma Z always said, "The Lord works in mysterious ways."

-30-

Leaving camp that year, Fred stole the Whammy and he displayed the ugly statue on a shelf in his house until the day he died. Some time after his death, Fred's wife Vivian, returned the Whammy to me. The stories instantly flooded back into my memory, and the Whammy now holds a hallowed spot on an office shelf in my home – much to my wife's chagrin. My wife never understood such things but I know that Uncle Dick, Brother Bob and my great friend Fred are smiling down from their lofty perches.

Chapter #11: A Time of Change

When preparing for high school graduation, most students have a plan for the future. I did not. I had turned down a scholarship in music because I wanted to be an engineer and work in the space program. However, no one offered me a science or engineering scholarship, and I had no desire to go into debt to enter college. When I returned from my survival pilgrimage to the Michigan north woods, I settled down as a writer/photographer for the Greenville Daily Advocate.

My Grandfather Light and my father had instilled the "code of journalism" in my mind at an early age. Unlike today, where ethics have little quarter in the field, there was a time when a set of unwritten rules guided the heart and soul of journalism. For example, if a true journalist wrote about a two-party controversy, he or she was obligated to write an even number of "he said" and "she said" quotes within any story that would appear on the front page or any other page in the newspaper, unless the story was written on the editorial page or in a private opinion column. I was very surprised when granddad told me that it was very important for a newspaper always to write an opinion about the controversy, and that, "It doesn't make any difference if the newspaper is Republican, Democrat or Communist."

"COMMUNIST," I thought. Granddad never had anything good to say about a communist. How could he believe it was okay if a newspaper in the United States of America was owned and operated by a communist? How could he think that any communistic opinion had value?

Looking back, Granddad Light was positively correct. You see, he had a positive outlook on the general intelligence of the average man or woman. He knew that bias of those owning a newspaper would be reasonably well known in the community. He also knew that if the unwritten journalistic rules were followed, the public would also have a good idea what each combatant in the controversy was thinking. When the reader added his own instinct to the mix, he or she usually could form an educated guess about that which he did and did not agree. Unfortunately, all journalism in today's fast-paced, hearsay-driven media is opinion backed by few facts and much bias.

My first foray into the daily newspaper world did not win me any awards or medals, but it did give me many new stories from which future generations might benefit. The following are but a few.

Story #49: Peacock or Poppycock

Life as a junior reporter/photographer for a small town newspaper is more social lesson than journalistic contribution. Mornings usually started with a walk about the downtown district where I would visit the local police department, fire department and county sheriff's office that was located in a poorly maintained jail building sitting adjacent to the impressive Darke County Court House.

Greenville seemed big to me since my primary experiences had been in tiny Fort Jefferson or the north woods. I was too busy playing music in the larger cities within the tri-state area, so my primary view of these cities was from inside the walls of nightclubs or from staring through the window of an auto as we traveled about.

Every weekday morning in fall of 1965, before the sun arose, I would make a beeline to the police department in order to have a cup of coffee with Chief Kelley. Chief Kelly was the classic picture of a storybook Irish cop. His large frame was covered with plenty of meat and he had a deep voice that boomed when he talked. His large-buttoned, deep blue uniform added to the image. I would take my time pawing through the sparse police reports, but more often, I would rely on Chief Kelly giving me the scoop on the previous day's activities.

One calm and mild morning, while downing a cup of coffee and chomping on a sweet roll, Chief Kelly's telephone range. He patiently waited for a second ring before lifting the phone to his ear and clearly enunciating, "Police department, Kelly speaking." This was followed by a lengthy pause, and then Kelly uttered, "Uh-huh ...... yep.... Okay ... uh-huh ... sure .... okay .... okay." Chief Kelly carefully returned the phone to the cradle and then shook his head. Looking my way he commented, "That was some loony woman in the city park. Said she had a peacock peering in her window. We get all kind of calls."

Chief Kelly and I had a good laugh. I peered out the window and noticed that the sun had arisen, which meant that I had spent more time eating and talking than working. I was about to leave the chief's office when his phone rang again. Again, Chief Kelly awaited the second ring before picking up. "Police department, Kelly speaking," he professed. "Yes ... yes ... where .... Okay ... uh-huh .... Hmmmm ... okay." His big right arm moved very slowly as he hung up the phone. He turned and stared at me a bit before saying, "That was another woman in the park saying there is a peacock looking in her window."

In the city of Greenville, Ohio, it would not be unusual to see a rabbit or perhaps a skunk wondering in the city park early in the morning. A possum would not be out of the question. A Cooper's hawk might be up and seeking an early rodent cuisine, but never had there been a peacock roaming within the city, or in the country for that matter.

Grandma Z used to say, "Truth is stranger than fiction," and as usual, she was correct. The two "crazy" women who called Chief Kelley also were correct. There was not just one peacock strolling around in the city park, there were many. The remainder of that pleasant fall day turned into a carnival.

There were peacocks chasing kids, there were kids chasing peacocks, there were policemen chasing kids and peacocks, there were dogs hunting peacocks, there were peacocks perched on houses, there were peacocks looking at their reflections in bedroom windows, there were women screaming at long-necked peeping Toms as the birds stared at their scantily clothed bodies, there were peacocks everywhere. God, it was great.

It's at times like this I think of Paul Harvey when he says, "Now you know the r-r-r-rest of the story." Yes, there is more to this story.

Do you remember Dwight Brown? He was the local orchestra director who gave me my first string bass. Mr. Brown also was Greenville's City Park Director. Mr. Brown had been on a trip to Europe where he had seen peacocks gently strolling in the beautifully manicured, stately parks. Secretly, he purchased a flock of peacocks and smuggled them into the city under the cloak of darkness. He stored them in the small metal building in the middle of the park while he planned the great unveiling. Ushering in a growth of sophistication for the local community was the goal. Unfortunately, (or fortunately for me), some high school students heard unusual sounds coming from the metal roost and freed the caged birds during the dark of night.

To this very day, peacocks still grace the town of Greenville; however, now they are imprisoned within a wire cage that was attached to the metal building. One cannot make up a story like this.

-30-

I remember with great admiration those in small communities who volunteered their services to better the city and its inhabitants. I met my fair share of these noble servants while working for the Advocate. I remember a young female dispatcher at the local sheriff department who worked under the guidance of James Irwin, Darke County's version of Andy of Mayberry. She later became a gifted city auditor for Greenville. Like Andy Taylor of Mayberry, Sheriff Irwin never needed to wear a firearm. I personally saw him walk into a local redneck bar and talk (without raising his voice) two "good ole' boys" (armed with broken bear bottles) out of killing one another. Then there was "Crib" Schlagetter, a salesmen-turned-mayor who never let his political party get in his way as he guided the city to a better future. The Greenville Daily Advocate gave all of these civil servants an open voice to the people when needed, but this was about to change.

The Brown family owned the local newspaper for many years and gave much back to their community. However, the times, they were a changing. In 1965, the family decided to sell the paper and there were no local buyers. The newspaper eventually was sold to Thompson Enterprises, a British newspaper conglomerate that was busily buying up a major share of small, locally owned newspapers in the United States.

Tempers became short in the newsroom as changes from afar were implemented without rhyme or reason. Most people of average sight can read 10 to 8 point type reasonably well. Classified ads used to be printed in very small 6-point type in order to get more ads on a page. Thompson said they wanted to get more news on a page, so they reduced the normal reading type to 7 point. Within a very short time, they then decided more white space was needed on a page, so margins were increased, which reduced the amount of type on the page. Now, Advocate customers could read less for two reasons: (1) The type required a magnifying glass, and (2) There were fewer words on the pages.

If this sounds irrational to you, you would be right. However, another major change to the newspaper was even worse. With no local ownership, it lost its community soul. Editorials became bland and without spirit. In Granddad Light's world, it was okay if a newspaper was Democratic, Republican or Communist-owned, as long as the unwritten rules were obeyed. Nevertheless, granddad could not have imagined a newspaper without a soul. Reading the Advocate became a lot like drinking warm water – you wanted to spat it out.

Due to gathering storm clouds at the newspaper and abroad in Viet Nam, it was time for a change. Something was driving me towards my dream of engineering, but college was still out of reach. Joining the military seemed like a viable option, so I approached a local U.S. Air Force recruiter to check out my options. I resigned from the Advocate, but there was a small problem. At the age of 13 months, I suffered from a serious heart disease (infectious endocarditis); however, the recent advent of a new wonder drug called penicillin pulled me through. Concurrently, I picked up the dreaded poliovirus that left me with the loss of a muscle in my right leg. I always felt quite lucky when I would be taken to Barney's Children's' Hospital in Dayton to be fitted with a bulky metal leg brace. Here I witnessed others who had been ravaged much more severely than I had. All male members of the Light family contracted polio at one time or another and Cousin Rush Light lost his life to the disease. When he was in high school, Dad was afflicted precisely the same as me, but he underwent a surgical procedure to rid himself of a brace. I was given the same opportunity, and at the age of ten, I was forced to learn how to walk again, but I became brace free for the first time in my walking life.

The Air Force recruiter never noticed my limp, and I scored high in the testing. When he offered me guaranteed training in electronics, I signed on the dotted line, but I also let the recruiter in on my dark secret.

"I don't think I can pass the physical," I admitted.

The recruiter leaned back in his chair and thought for a minute. "Do you think you could pass a draft physical?" he asked.

"I don't know, "I said. "I have never been through one."

I was amazed. Here was a perfect stranger who was willing to risk his job in order to help me.

The recruiter set up an appointment for a draft physical in Columbus, Ohio. There were hundreds of young men being given Army physicals and it was an easy matter to cover up the deficiency with my right leg. Within one week, I was on my way to Lackland Air Force Base near San Antonio, Texas.

I apologize for this rather lengthy explanation, but I believe it will better let you understand the stories you are about to read.

Story #50: The Greeting

It was late evening when the old bus drove through the rather stark entrance gate to Lackland Air Force Base. There was little conversation on the bus as most of us were deeply entranced with confusion and some degree of fear. We came from everywhere. We were of various colors and sizes, and we were separated by a more-or-less common language.

The deafening silence was shattered when a man in uniform entered the bus and shouted, "Out, out of the bus and line up single file behind the white line to your left."

We quickly complied and shuffled into the requested line formation. A rigid-looking sergeant then began to bark out instructions in a cadence that sounded more like a machine gun than a human voice. My mind was able to interpret about one out of every 10 words, but as the chatter continued, the message became clearer. Suddenly, without warning, he challenged, "If there is anyone in this line that thinks he can whip me, I want him to step out of line now."

There was a brief moment of silence, and then a muscular recruit, who stood about 6'5" in height, stepped out of the line, yet remained at attention. The sergeant stared at the recruit and then ordered, "Walk this way." When the recruit arrived at the sergeant's location, the sergeant directed him to turn around and stand beside him. Without any hesitation, the sergeant then addressed the remainder of us saying, "This, gentlemen, will be your group leader. If anyone in this line thinks he can whip the two or us, step out of the line now." There were no volunteers.

-30-

My introduction to military life was not what I expected. Clearly, this was a place of discipline, wit and wisdom. What was to come would give me great faith in and respect for our military but also would cause me great frustration.

Story #51: I'm Superman

Without question, I was one of a few odd men in the honor flight to which I was assigned. With the war in Viet Nam raging, many of those entering the Air Force were doing so to avoid the draft. I wanted to earn an education and learn more about the world. How the Air Force was going to forge us into a crack fighting or support unit was beyond my imagination.

The barracks at Lackland were large, two-story, wood-framed structures, each of which housed an entire flight. Upon entering the two-door front entry, we were greeted with a restroom on the left and a wide wooden staircase that led to the second story. Bunk beds lined both

sides of the two stories, and a single office for the staff and tech sergeants was located at the top of the stairway on the left. On the office door that insulated the sergeants from the recruits, was painted a red hand. At the far end of the upper story was a set of double doors that led to a small wooden balcony. On the end outside wall at each side of the balcony stood two narrow wooden ladders that were to be used as fire escapes.

All in all, it did not seem like a bad place to reside. Stowing gear and listening to the never-ending instructions took us into the early hours of morning. Finally, it was time to hit the sack and await revelry. No sooner had I dozed off, when a fire alarm sounded and we all were herded outside. It was determined to be a false alarm, so we all returned to our beds. That night saw no less than five fire alarms, each of which forced us out of the barracks. When the recorded bugle sounded in the morning, all of us were in a trance.

Day two at basic training is a blur in my mind, but night two is as clear as a bell in my memory. Again, we suffered though five fire drills that repeatedly interrupted our sleep. By day three, we were all so focused on staying awake and complaining about fire drills that our many differences no longer seemed important.

We all expected more fire drills on night three, so I decided to stay awake until the first one was over. My mind was racing through a myriad of thoughts when the silence in the darkened barracks was broken by a young recruit directly opposite my bunk. He jumped to his feet on top of his bed and yelled, "I'm Superman!" He then leaped from the bed, and ran at full speed for the length of the second-story barracks, then launched himself -- head first -- off the balcony. After a brief flight in his underwear and without a cape, he plunged two stories and crashed into the grass below.

Several of us scampered down the flimsy wooden ladders to find "Superman" laughing as he cradled his broken ankle between his hands. "This was a pretty rude awakening," he explained. He was rushed to the base hospital and later was transferred to casual barracks until he healed.

-30-

At first, I was disturbed that sleep deprivation had caused an injury to one of my fellow soldiers. However, as time passed, I was amazed how the Air Force was able to get a group of diverse and self-centered young men to work together as a collective group toward a noble end. Today, there are factions in our society who are hell bent to eliminate all risk from our daily lives. The search for the elimination of all risk is a fool's folly. I have learned that some degree of measured risk is required to obtain the noblest causes. Without some degree of risk and sacrifice, advancement to a higher calling is virtually impossible.

Story #52: Little Big Man

It has never been clear to me how I ended up in an honor flight at Lackland. My fellow recruits and I seemed quite average to me, but our staff and tech sergeants made it clear that we were indeed an honor flight, and they would insure that we would not damage their reputations.

Life in basic training was very busy and directed. Our sergeants repeatedly explained the rules and made sure that our physical conditioning improved. Calisthenics several times a day were interrupted by house cleaning chores and education in rules and regulations.

Our staff and tech sergeants were as different as night and day. Staff Sergeant Kelley was more reserved and generally wore a smile. Our tech sergeant was a man of small stature who was regimented in his personality and his actions.

The red right hand painted on the sergeants' office door was a target for our right hands to apply a singular smack in order to gain an audience with one or both sergeants. My bunk was situated directly opposite the office door, and time after time, I would hear a sharp crack followed by a voice from the opposite side of the door singing, "I can't ♫ hear you." This brought about a second loud "crack" followed by a second, "I can't ♫ hear you." Sometimes, it would take four or five raps on the red hand before the rapper would be allowed to enter the inner sanctum.

Revelry sounded at its normal early hour one rare rainy morning. Normally, we would have been ushered out of the building for calisthenics, but this day was different. Even the sergeants had no desire to brave the downpour. Therefore, our entire flight slid all bunks on the second-story against the outer walls to form a miniature gymnasium. Sergeant Kelley was barking out the commands while the tech sergeant observed our individual performances. During one break in the activities, a muffled voice emitting from the back of the honor flight announced, "I don't see him doing any of these exercises."

Yes, we were trying to learn military tactics, but clearly, Private Johnson made a tactical error.

"Johnson!" the tech sergeant barked. "Front and center, now!"

Johnson worked his way through the flight and then stood facing Sarge.

"Here's what we're going to do," Sarge explained. "I am going to do one-handed push-ups and you are going to do two-handed push-ups. For every one-handed push-up I do more than your two-handed push-ups, you will do 50 push-ups at my digression at any place and any time."

Johnson was not a weakling, so most of us thought Sarge's mind might be writing checks his body could not cash. Nevertheless, down to the floor both men went and the duel was on. You might think there would have been loud cheering in the barracks as the battle was joined, but you could have heard a humming bird cough. Up and down and up and down and up and down and up and down they went.

Johnson's face began to turn red and his cadence began to slow. Sarge's rigid frame continued to oscillate with no reduction in pace and no indication of fatigue. Eventually, Johnson fell flat on the floor, but the tech sergeant's one-armed water pump imitation continued unabated. When Johnson fell by the way, our flight instinctively started counting in unison, aloud. We have no way of knowing what was going through Johnson's mind, but my guess is that he was multiplying each number we would chant by 50.

Fifty extra push-ups later, the tech sergeant hopped to his feet, seemingly no worse for wear, and asked Sergeant Kelley to resume calisthenics. Johnson, with head down, returned to his place at the rear of the flight.

For the remainder of my stay at Lackland, it was a common sight to see airman Johnson doing 50 push-ups at various odd locations on the base with the tech sergeant looking on with a pleasant smile on his face.

-30-

I have often heard those who have never served in the armed forces criticize our military. They cynically claim that "military intelligence" is an oxymoron, even though they have no firsthand knowledge of the demands put upon our military leaders and soldiers. It is my very considered opinion that those who routinely criticize the military services of the United States are fools and elitists. My brief experience in the Air Force gave me a great respect for those who care enough about our nation and the freedom that it enjoys to willingly risk their lives so future generations might share in these freedoms.

Story #53: Those Damn Shoes

I must admit, it took me about two weeks before beginning to understand the logic behind the "abusive" training tactics. It was a very surreal world, but in a very short period, I made friends more quickly than I ever had. My family, fearing I would become dependent due to the polio leg, raised me to be independent and self-sufficient. At Lackland, I was learning that it was okay to put trust in others as long as the common goal was justified towards the benefit of all humankind.

My feelings were good as our flight was marched to a building where we were to be issued uniforms. You quickly get used to standing in long lines in the military, and this morning was no exception. All was well until our barefooted flight formed single file for our shoes issue. The line moved along quickly, and I could see one man after another being handed shiny black footwear.

When I arrived at the front of the line, my heart sank. In front of me stood a threat not anticipated. I was ordered to step upon a contraption where a bar was run up against my toes in order to measure the length of my feet. Polio had left me with a right foot that was two inches shorter than my left, and the bar told no lies.

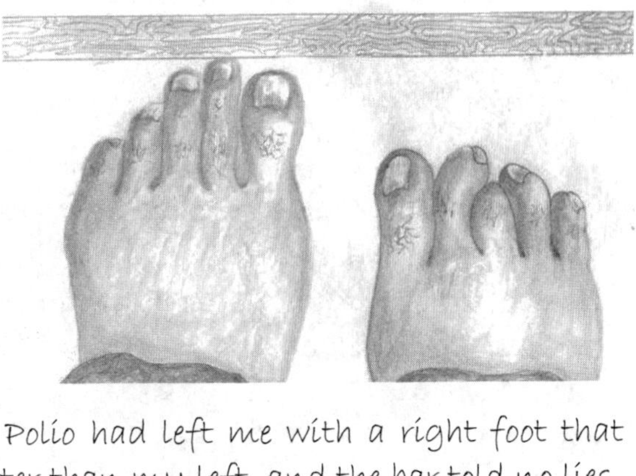

"Step out of line," ordered the measurement airman.

"Why, sir?" I questioned.

"I said step out of line," he repeated.

"Why, sir?" I demanded.

"Because, we cannot issue special shoes," he reasoned.

"I do not require special shoes, sir. I walked into this man's Air Force with shoes just like yours, sir," I explained.

"Step out of line, now!" he barked.

As we marched back to the barracks, I was the only airman wearing civilian shoes. My dark secret had been uncovered and my spirits were at an all-time low. My sergeants said nothing, but the next morning I received orders to report to the base hospital that afternoon. I had no idea how to fight the indignity as I sat on my bed and stared at the red hand on the door. I felt intense anger, but I could not decide whom to hate. My sergeants were in their office and I was alone in the barracks.

I mustered the courage to approach the office door, a place where I had feared to approach in weeks past. "They're going to hear me," I thought.

Being a part-time farm worker in my youth, and very recently living off the land in northern Michigan for a month, put me in peak physical condition. I reached back with my right arm, and with all my strength I slammed my hand into the red hand on the office door. The panel upon which the red hand was painted gave way with a loud crack, and the momentum of my blow caused me to fall through the gaping hole, my body hanging in an awkward position, suspended by my waist.

"Come in," Sergeant Kelley said in a surprisingly calm voice.

Unhooking myself from the door, I picked up the wooden panel that laid in front of the large metal desk.

"Please put that on my desk and sit down," Sgt. Kelley continued. "What's on your mind?"

When I explained to Sarge that I wanted to remain in the Air Force, he asked numerous questions, and then said, "Would you like me to go with you in the morning and talk to the doctors?"

"Yes, sir," I said.

Things did not go as planned. The next morning I was summarily admitted to the hospital, and there I spent a full week undergoing an unbelievable battery of tests. There was not a spot on my body or head that avoided inspection. Eventually I was sent to casual barracks, a place where airmen await being shipped back to civilian life. While awaiting my disposition, one of my fellow causal barracks inmates committed suicide by cutting his wrists during the night. To say depression had set in would be a gross understatement of my feelings at the time. "Those damn shoes," I thought.

Three days later, Sergeant Kelley appeared at my door and said, "Come on Light. You and I are going to visit the head doctor."

When we reached the hospital, we were granted an audience, and Sarge did an eloquent job pleading my case.

Looking over his thick, dark-rimmed glasses, the physician stared directly at me and challenged, "What would you do if we had to drop you into a jungle in the middle of Viet Nam?"

"Sir," I replied, "I just lived off the land in the forests of northern Michigan for over a month armed only with a bow and knife. How many of these other airmen have done that?"

What followed was a crisp point and counterpoint argument between the doctor and Sarge and me. Eventually, it became obvious that the doctor's decision had been made long before we entered his office.

Sarge and I returned to his office. "Do you want to carry this to another level?" he asked.

"What are my chances, Sarge?"

"Not good. Not good at all," he stated, "But, I will back you if you want to go on."

For the first time in my life, I felt utterly defeated. It was not a good feeling. At the same time, I felt great pride in knowing some of the best men I had ever encountered. I had been privileged to participate in one of the greatest organizations in the world, and I knew it.

Two days later, I received my honorable discharge paperwork, and I was sitting on a Boeing 707 heading for home. My seat was at the rear of the plane and I felt very alone. My newfound friends were behind me and I knew that it was unlikely that I would ever see any of them again. When the plane landed in Chicago, I rushed to my connecting flight to Dayton, Ohio. Much to my surprise, there standing in line was the publisher of the Greenville Daily Advocate, the newspaper where I had resigned such a short time before.

"You on leave already?" he asked.

"No sir, I have been mustered out."

"Your job is still open if you want it," he offered.

"Sure," I said. "Thanks."

-30-

Homecoming was a quiet affair. In small towns, even in bigger cities like Greenville, rumors run rampant. It wasn't long before it was being reported that I had deliberately skipped out of military service to avoid the war in Viet Nam. It was bad enough that the Air Force found me unfit for service, but to be accused of that which was farthest from my mind was most disturbing. To this very day, I harbor unresolved questions regarding my decision not to take Sergeant Kelley up on his most kind offer. Even though my military service lasted weeks instead of years, it feels good to know that I was a part of a proud and honorable profession. When attending high school choir presentations at the stately Memorial Hall in Greenville, I feel a deep obligation to stand when the kids sing the armed services' medley.

Story #54: Have Bass, Will Travel

Things at the Greenville Daily Advocate had not changed much since I left for my career in the Air Force. Thompson Enterprises still owned the business and policy was wishy-washy with no clear direction.

The old editorial staff was still there. Bill still held the managing editor's position; Jim covered city politics, while Susie covered the society scene. I went back to covering the police, sheriff and fire beat and shot a few pictures. It was still a full-time job, but I had a nagging dissatisfaction that could not be defined – only felt. I dearly enjoyed my working associates, but my mind constantly drifted and dreamed when it should have been focused on work.

Darke County was primarily a German community; however, the French founded a small village located north of Greenville. The Germans apparently had an influence over the French in the early days because the village was named Versailles, but became pronounced "Ver-sales" instead of "Fairsigh," as it was in France. Located slightly outside of Versailles sat a most remarkable facility known as the Crystal Ballroom - a huge, sprawling building that sat in the middle of a cornfield, and a place where the best big bands in the country came to perform. Couples drove many miles to dance their nights away under a giant, sparkling, mirror-covered orb that dangled above the spacious wooden dance floor.

Jimmy Baltes, a short Frenchman and avid drummer, led the house band for the Crystal. Jimmy was not the best technical drummer in the world, but he had a God-given talent to play rhythms to which people would dance for hours and hours. While aspiring to become a musician, I frequently would travel to the Crystal where Jimmy would allow me to sit in with the band. He did not care whether I played piano, string bass or trumpet. Jimmy always felt like family.

Sitting at my newspaper office desk one day, I noticed that the famous Si Zentner Orchestra, a 22-piece big band, was going to be performing at the Crystal on Saturday night. The Si Zentner Orchestra had reached the top of the charts with the hit arrangement of "Up the Lazy River," featuring Si's magnificent trombone virtuosity. I called two friends, and we decided to go together for the Saturday extravaganza. Besides, at the Crystal, an 18-year-old like me could drink 3/2 beer without fear of arrest.

The show was great, but my mood was not. I have no idea how many bottles of 3/2 beer I drank, but something bolstered my courage. As I sat listening to the band, it suddenly struck me that I could play bass equal to or better than the bass player on the Si Zentner Orchestra. When I walked to the back of the bandstand, I could see the bass player's sheet music, and it looked less complicated than the charts I routinely played with Johnny McCoy's band.

Returning to the table, I pulled out my musician's union card and borrowed a felt-tip pen.

Before I go on with the story, I want to remind you that when young, I always wanted to be a cowboy or an Indian. Vestiges of these desires continued into my teenage years. One television show I watched religiously was "Paladin," a western starring Richard Boone, who played a sophisticated gunman for hire. His business card read: "HAVE GUN - WILL TRAVEL."

I took the felt-tipped pin, and in bold print scribed "HAVE BASS – WILL TRAVEL" on my union card. Then I waited for the band to take a break. When the band members exited the stage, only Si Zentner remained to call up the next set of tunes. There was only one way for Si to leave the Crystal's bandstand, and I blocked that exit. When Si approached, I raised up the union card in front of his face. Si smiled and then laughed aloud.

"Do you play," he asked.

"Yep," I said.

"Do you read," he quizzed.

"Better than him," I stated while nodding towards Si's current bass player.

"Who have you played with?" he said.

"Johnny McCoy," I replied.

Si handed my union card back to me, and I stepped aside so he could go out to meet the appreciative audience. I returned to my table, where my friends and I had a great laugh. We stayed at the Crystal for two more sets then left without saying another word to Si Zentner.

-30-

Neither before nor after my encounter with Si Zentner did I again execute such a self-centered, public exhibition. It is funny what 3/2 beer can do to a young man.

Story #55: Sure, Right!

It was ten o'clock at night, and I was upstairs in our 200-year-old bedroom preparing to sleep. I heard the faint sound of the telephone ringing in the downstairs kitchen.

"It's for you," mom yelled up the stairway.

It wasn't unusual to receive calls at 10 PM, so I jogged down the stairs and picked up the phone.

"Hello," I puffed

In the earpiece, I heard a distant voice say, "Is this Bill?"

"Yes," I responded.

"This is Si Zentner," came the reply.

My friends were good friends, and as such, we frequently played practical jokes on each other. Therefore, I knew that the voice on the other end of the phone was either Greg or Mike.

"Sure, right!" I said.

There was a pregnant pause on the other end of the phone. I cannot remember exactly what happened next, but the voice on the other end of the phone was Si Zentner and he was calling me from Las Vegas.

After I apologized for my rather strange greeting, Si asked, "Do you still want to play in my band?"

"When do you need to know?" I questioned.

"I must know by tomorrow night," he said. "You must call me by tomorrow night."

Wow! I could not believe my ears, but still I felt obligated to be responsible, even though I really had no idea what that meant. Si gave me his phone number, and I promised that I would call him at 6 p.m. the next day, Las Vegas time.

It took a while to get to sleep that night due to worry about what my parents and Editor Bill would think if I resigned a second time from the Advocate.

The next morning came early, so before Dad left for work, I explained what I was contemplating. He gave no response or recommendation. His lack of response made me nervous. Dad and I both left for our full-time jobs.

When I arrived at the Advocate that morning, I requested a meeting with Bill. I explained my situation and then awaited his response. It was not what I expected.

"This is an once-in-a-lifetime opportunity for you," he offered. "If I were you, I would do it." Then he quietly but candidly added, "I doubt that any of us in the editorial staff will still be here when you come back for a visit."

I thanked Bill for his advice and turned in my resignation. I finished the day at work, cleared out my desk and headed for home to face my parents.

"Dad," I said with reservation, "I have decided to join the Si Zentner Orchestra."

Without hesitation Dad responded, "I would have done precisely the same thing if I were you." Then, he smiled – a smile that was worth more to me than all the money in Fort Knox.

I called Si that night, and two days later, I received two airline tickets (one for me and one for my bass) to Las Vegas, Nevada. Included with the tickets was an itinerary that defined the adventure of my life.

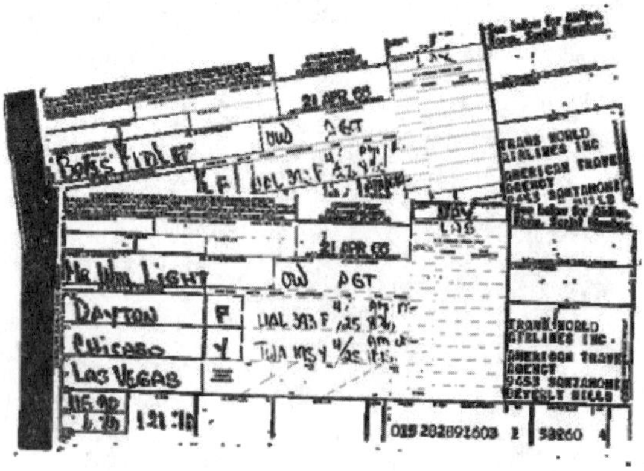

Chapter #12: Road Life

If someone had told me I would some day be sitting in a jet airplane heading for Las Vegas to play string bass for one of the top big bands in the country, I would have thought he was crazy. Who could have figured that 3/2 beer would be a factor in such a world-shaking occurrence. Nevertheless, it was not a dream. Just think of it, a would-be cowboy and/or Indian, farm hand, veterinarian assistant, rocketeer, newspaper writer/photographer, musician, and short-term airman was heading to the Tropicana to open as a bass player behind the marvelous talents of none other than Mel Torme.

Story #56: Coffee, Tea or Me?

People looked on with curiosity as I hefted my large string bass upon my right shoulder and walked across the Dayton Municipal Airport tarmac towards the metal steps that led up to a waiting Boeing 707 jet passenger plane. I dodged my way along the narrow isle inside the craft and then belted my bass into the window seat facing the forward bulkhead. I parked myself in the aisle seat beside the bass.

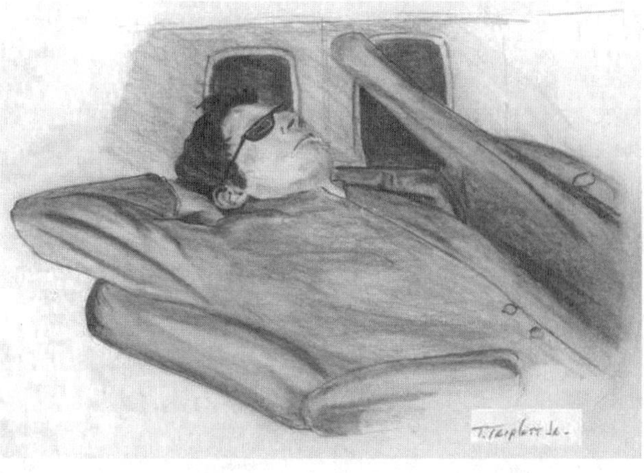

My mind was running in overdrive; however, I tried very hard to look cool. "Cool" was a word often used by musicians in those days. It ranked right up there with "hip, get down, and funky." It was also important to look the part, so I wore a Nehru jacket and jet-age dark glasses.

This was only my second time aboard a jet aircraft, but I knew it would not be cool to allow anyone else to know. Shortly the plane lifted off, and soon we departed from Dayton air space.

One stewardess aboard the plane caught my eye. She was quite beautiful, and she looked to be about my age. She walked my way and introduced herself.

"Who's your friend," she asked.

"Oh that's my old girl," I said with a smile.

"She's got quite a figure. Have you known her long?" she asked.

I really wanted to say something like, "Her figure isn't anything like yours;" however, at that very moment I had the strange feeling that a family member was looking over my shoulder.

"I've only known her for a few months, but she's great with a conversation," I said.

The attractive flight attendant smiled and then returned to her duties.

That was fun, I thought. Then, I tilted my seat backwards and closed my eyes. The flight was only about half full, and there were empty seats across the aisle from me. I must have dozed off because it seemed like only a few minutes had passed when someone tugged at my sleeve. I looked over to see the pleasant stewardess sitting across from me.

"Would you like to talk a bit," she said.

What I wanted to say was, "Are you kidding?" Instead, I simply said, "Sure."

We talked about things. I have no idea what things we talked about because I was much too busy admiring her numerous visual gifts. One thing led to another, and, of course, I told her that I was a big band road musician just on my way to Las Vegas to help my good friend Si Zentner. Okay, so Si wasn't my good friend yet, but she didn't know that.

Time, quite literally, flew by. Before I knew it, I asked the young lady if she was doing anything in the morning and suggested that we could have breakfast together. To my surprise and total delight, she accepted my invitation. She recommended a nice breakfast nook on the strip, and I agreed to meet here there at 8 A.M., Las Vegas time.

When we landed, I unloaded my bass, picked up my solitary piece of luggage, and headed for the hotel. Had I looked a little closer at the itinerary that Si had sent, I might have noticed that the opening job was <u>not</u> at the Tropicana with Mel Torme. The Torme gig had already occurred. If I had known a bit more about the habits of big bands, I might have known that most of the big bands formed up in Las Vegas prior to going on cross-country road trips. Had I known a little more about dating beautiful young women, perhaps I would have requested the address or phone number of the beautiful stewardess. The truth is that none of those things ever crossed my mind.

When I arrived at my hotel, things occurred at a torrid pace. First, there was the task of procuring proper band attire, including multiple gaudy jackets. Then, it was get-acquainted-with-some-of-the-musicians time, and then came the surprise of my life. Si explained that all should meet in front of the hotel and board the bus at 6 A.M. sharp. It was at that exact moment that I remembered the lovely stewardess who would be awaiting my company at the breakfast nook along the Las Vegas strip at 8 A.M. the next morning. "Oh God," I thought, "How could I get into this predicament?"

I boarded the bus the next morning, and I was assigned two seats as my new home. I was lucky because a married man traveling with his wife had to share two seats.

It was very quiet that morning. As the bus pulled away from the hotel, few people talked, and those that did talked in whispers. Most of the veterans simply fell asleep. I sat and dreamed about a relationship that was not meant to be.

-30-

Over the years, I wondered what happened to the beautiful young flight attendant. I told my story to several close friends. Numerous years ago, one of these friends excitedly said to me, "Have you seen that new book called 'Coffee, Tea or Me'?"

"No, I haven't," I admitted.

"Your story is in there," he said.

"What story?" I asked.

"The one about the stewardess," he explained.

He was correct. I never had the courage to write to the author of the book. As sure as I am writing these stories, this author was indeed the beautiful and charming flight attendant that I abandoned in Las Vegas. It truly is a small world.

Story #57: Rolling Home Away from Home

By the time the sun arose, our big Greyhound-like bus was well out of Vegas, and this was the first time I clearly saw the faces of my fellow musicians and a few road wives. It also was the first time I saw the bus driver – a good-sized, barrel-chested man named Ray Fay. Ray was the owner of the LaGrange Bus Line in Illinois, but also he was a great fan of big bands. Consequently, he decided to spend

Ray Fay and Rolling Home Away from Home

months piloting our band bus back and forth across the lower 48 states.

Si and Ray were kindred spirits. Si Zentner was raised in the New York Bronx, and his mother made him take violin lessons. Unfortunately for Si, his teacher lived several blocks away, and he had to walk to the lessons through hostile streets. You had to be a very tough kid to carry a violin case anywhere in the Bronx, and Si was tough. When Si reached adulthood, he drove large trucks for a living, and he willingly shared the band bus driving requirements with Ray during our road tour. This meant that, if needed, our bus could be driven 24 hours a day, and sometimes it was needed.

I stared out the window at the desert view and watched the cactus fly by a brake-neck speed. I really didn't know anyone. In fact, my only association with Si was the brief comic encounter at the Crystal Ballroom. Living in the two-seat "home" behind me was Rod Adams, a free-spirited tenor sax man with a marvelous sense of humor.

Breaking the silence, I turned around and asked Rod, "Hey man, how did Zentner get enough money to start a big band?"

"He's a millionaire," Rod offered.

"Wow! Did he make that much money from Up a Lazy River?" I queried. Up a Lazy River had reached the top of the charts a couple of years before I joined the band.

"Not hardly," Rod frowned. "He made it by going from movie studio to movie studio during the hay days."

"Is he really that good?"

"He plays great and he really reads well," Rod replied. "I have seen him read and play difficult and high trumpet parts on that trombone."

I was impressed! A voice from across the aisle joined the conversation.

"I hear you come from Ohio," a rather tall, thin dude injected. "Where yuh from?"

"Greenville, Ohio," I said. "It's a town located about......"

"I know," the thin man interrupted. "My name is Johnny Landecker and my wife and I are from Dayton. I'm the drummer."

I could not believe it. Here I was, cruising down the highway in the middle of Nevada with a bunch of strangers and the second guy I officially meet came from just a few miles down the road. His quiet and beautiful wife leaned forward in her seat and smiled.

Then a voice from behind me yelled, "I'm from Ohio too."

"Where?" I shouted back.

"Arntun," he replied.

"Ironton?" I questioned.

"Yep. My name's Mel..... Mel Kunkle...bari sax."

"Do you know Johnny McCoy?" I asked.

"Hell yes! Played with him some. One tough son-of-a-bitch," he offered.

I immediately knew two things for sure. Mel was from Ironton because only the locals call it "Arntun," and he surely did know Johnny McCoy. I felt right at home.

-30-

I do not know what the odds of meeting two road musicians from my home area out of a 22-man band, but my guess is that it is not normal. I always thought that most professional musicians hailed from New York City, Las Vegas, New Orleans or Los Angeles. As I was to learn, a major share of big band musicians came from rather remote rural areas.

For a young man who was used to sleeping on open ground in the north woods, living within the confines of two large, soft seats on a moving bus seemed quite comfortable. Why the older musicians complained about the cramped quarters made no sense to me whatsoever.

The memories of gazing out the window at the great expanse of open desert as Ray guided the vehicle down the highway at 70+ miles per hour are as clear today as they were 40 years ago. My mind drifted from imagining the future to enjoying the scenery, to remembering friends and family, and wishing that they could share the adventure with me.

My life with the Si Zentner Orchestra generated more stories than I could possibly write in one book. We crisscrossed the country several times, generally playing one-night stands and occasionally playing a month-long gig at

Lake Tahoe or Vegas. It was a very physical job, and there was little time for activities outside our small bus community. I hope that the following snippets in time will help you better understand the life of a road musician.

Story #58: The Games We Play

Rod Adams was a fine tenor sax player. He had a natural kindness and a keen wit that could be as sharp as a fine hunting knife. Rod lived in a two-seated "house" directly behind mine. It has never been clear to me whether it was the close proximity of our two bus abodes, or a special affinity that we had for one another, but whatever the reasons, Rod and I got along with each other quite well.

After several weeks on the road, humor seemed to be the glue that kept Rod and me amicable. With others, the length of patience seemed to be inversely proportional to length of the endless highway. It was not unusual for high-volume arguments to erupt on the bus without warning. Our keyboard player carried a miniature piano keyboard with him on the bus, and he spent hours practicing scales. Unfortunately, the keyboard clicked with each key stroke.

As time went by, this sound took on all of the warmth of children scratching their fingernails across a grade school blackboard. Our piano man was not our most popular musician.

For Rod and me, bus life was a time to hone our comedic skills. Generally, it was a time to retell stories, jokes, or a combination of both. At one point, I remember coming to the conclusion that all original jokes must have originated with road musicians or prison convicts. Surely, I thought, only in these boring environments was there adequate time available to create such masterpieces. Rod was particularly good at coming up with original jokes. Over the many years that followed, routinely someone would tell me a joke that Rod had invented. For example, the following is a Rod Adams original:

"An Indian tribe in the Great Plains had been confined on a reservation by self-serving white men. The Chief of the tribe had a vision in which the Great Spirit instructed him to send his young son to white man's school in order to learn the way of the whites and, in turn, better the tribe and lift it out of the dust-filled poverty of the reservation. The Chief explained the vision to the tribal elders, and all of the reservation inhabitants donated their worldly possessions to raise enough money to send the boy to school. The Chief's son worked hard for many years. He finally was graduated with a bachelor's degree in electrical engineering. He returned to the reservation where he planned to repay the debt he owed his family and tribe. He walked about the reservation in search of a vision that would help him repay the debt. However, what could an electrical engineer possibly do? Week passed. Then one night he saw that which would change his life. He noticed that when old *squaws would head to the out tee pees for relief; many times, they would trip along the trail due to the darkness and failing eyesight. The next day, the young Indian engineer began purchasing large spools of wire, tall lodge poles, an electrical generator, powerful lights, and all sorts of other electrical equipment. For many weeks, he worked erecting the poles, stringing the wires and connecting the lights. Then he asked the Tribal Council to gather the tribe for a very special night. When the tribe was gathered around the council fire, the young engineer asked his aged father to throw the ceremonial switch. When the switch was thrown, lights throughout the reservation illuminated the pathways to the out-house tee pees, and the old squaws cheered with delight."*

-30-

Now, I am very much aware that you probably are a bit disgruntled. I fully understand that you probably feel cheated in that you didn't find Rod's story very funny. Perhaps it would help you to know that the young Indian engineer was actually a very famous figure in history. You see, this young engineer was **"the first man ever to wire a head for a reservation**." Now you know the rest of the story.

I know, some of you still just don't get it. You see, "head" is a sailor's term for a toilet. Sheesh, I really hate it when I have to explain a good joke.

I will relate another Rod Adams piece of humor a bit later in another story, but first I would like you to meet Milt Yaner, whom I affectionately remember as Uncle Milty.

Story #59: Uncle Milty

The Si Zentner Orchestra was not just one entity. In fact, the Si Zentner Orchestra made most of its recordings using various studio musicians who were collected by Si at the time the recordings were made. The real Si Zentner Orchestra consisted of Si Zentner and a book of extremely good big band arrangements. When the band went on the road, Si would hire musicians who he knew to be capable readers and players.

When our road band formed up in Vegas, our trombone section was superb, our trumpet section was excellent, our drummer was great, and our sax section had four talented players who did not play well as a group.

Si Zentner was not a man to tolerate mediocrity, so job security was always questionable. It wasn't long before we suffered our first casualty. Si fired the lead alto-sax-man, and immediately replaced him with a short, white-haired, Yiddish man named Milt Yaner. Since Si also was of Jewish heritage, I figured the selection was natural.

Milt hailed from New York City, and for many years he was the first chair sax man for the Radio City Music Hall orchestra – which in its day was the pinnacle for musicianship. Unfortunately, Milt had a taste for alcohol and became, by his own admission, a lush. He put his life back in order shortly before joining our band and was completely "straight" all of the time I knew him.

Milt's kindly demeanor and small stature belied a strong determination, a great love of music, and a drive for professionalism. Milt's leadership roped in the other three sax individuals, and within one week, we had one of the top sax sections in the world.

Perhaps, it was my young age, or maybe it was my country ways, that told Milt that I could use some help. About the second day on the bus, Milt strolled back to my house, looked around, and questioned, "Where's your shoebox?"

The question took me aback. "What?" I returned.

"Your shoebox! Where in the hell is it?" Milt barked.

"What shoebox?" I asked.

"The shoebox you keep your receipts in," he said.

"What bills?" I posed.

"All of your bills. Where in the hell were you raised?" he continued. "You gotta have a shoebox. You're a musician now! Are you gonna buy a record player?"

"Maybe," I answered.

"Training......it's deductible," Milt instructed. "You gonna buy any clothing?"

"Probably," I responded.

"You're a show person now. It's part of your shtik," he continued. "It's deductible."

I had never heard the word "shtik" before, and so I had to play cool and act as if I had some idea what Milt was talking about. It also was clear to me that if I didn't get a shoebox and I didn't put all of my receipts in it, Milt would never let me hear the end of it. The next day, I purchased a new pair of shiny back shoes, just so I would have my own shoebox.

-30-

Milt Yaner was more than a fine musician. He was more than a good friend. Milt was a real human being who had a wonderful outlook on life. He was only the second Jewish man (the first was Si) that I had ever had time to get to know. I liked both Milt and Si and they taught me much, but more importantly, they gained my respect and showed me that people from very different backgrounds have more in common than not.

Story #60: The War

It was uncommonly quiet on the bus as it pulled away from the job site. It had not been one of our better performances. There had been some open resistance to Si's authority and judgment on the bandstand. It was not noticeable to the audience, but it had gotten Si's attention. And, when Si was unhappy, everyone was unhappy.

In the front of the bus, I saw Si pop the cork on a bottle of J&B whiskey, and then down a couple of slugs. One time I had asked Si why he liked J&B whiskey. He responded simply saying with a smile, "Jewish booze."

It was about 2 a.m. and most of us simply wanted to fall asleep. Apparently, Milt Yaner had other ideas. Ray piloted the bus down the darkened streets; the amplitude of the voices in the front of the bus grew. Si and Milt were standing toe-to-toe, face-to-face and nose-to-nose in the isle, and both were shouting as loud as they possibly could; however, the pace was so quick that the words were unintelligible.

The argument raged for minutes – not seconds. All expected the two "old men" to start landing punches, or at least wrestle each other to the floor. Then, at some preordained time, a deafening silence ensued after Si shouted, "You could be back on the street."

Both men instantly turned and sat down on their respective seats. The only time in my life that I ever experienced such a silence was when I spent a night alone in an up-ground swamp in Michigan. It was precisely at this time when a haunting whistle from the seat directly behind mine could be heard over the low-pitched drone of the bus.

For those of you not musically inclined, this is the theme melody from the western movie called "Hi Noon" starring Gary Cooper. The words in this phrase are, "Do not forsake me oh my darling."

Needless to say, Si Zentner immediately recognized the theme because he had played in the band that recorded the music for the movie, and Si was not pleased! He leaped to his feet and headed down the bus isle repeatedly shouting, "Who whistled that!"

As he approached the back of the bus, Rod quietly raised his hand and calmly stated, "I cannot tell a lie, it was I."

Si's face was glowing red as he stared at Rod. Then he shouted, "I might have known it would be you, smartass."

With that pronouncement, Si stormed back down the aisle to his seat. The silence hung in the air like a dark sheet. No one spoke another word that night.

-30-

Our big band was a collection of one of the most diverse groups of humanity that one can envision. To perform at this level required not only some musical talent but also the ability for persons with profoundly different drives and personalities to find ways to achieve a common goal at a professional level. More importantly, the performances always must be at a level that audiences find enjoyable and exciting.

There were conflicts occurring nearly every day; however, when the curtain would rise, the musicians put all battles aside and performance was the name of the game. During my first three weeks on the road, my fingers on both hands would bleed profusely after each performance. I learned to soak them in vinegar to toughen the skin. By the time I ended my professional musical career, the fingernail on my right index finger had rotated until it rested vertically on the right side of my finger. The fingernail on my second finger resided at a 45-degree angle. The hide covering these fingers was rigid enough to cause a wine glass to ring when struck by one or the other.

I met and was privileged to accompany many celebrities over the years, and quickly learned who were good human beings, and who were stuck on themselves. One of my all-time favorite human beings was Barbara McNair, a most lovely singer whose hit single -- "The Shadow of Your Smile" -- made the top ten lists. Barbara later starred in movies. I first met Barbara while playing for a coming-out party sponsored by Henry Ford II.

The next story altered significantly my perceptions of culture in the United States. Barbara and her heritage are a part of this story.

Story #61: Two Nights to Remember

I should have known that the earth was going to shift on its axis. Just one night before, Si fired our piano player immediately following a performance at Indiana University. It wasn't as if the piano player had deliberately sabotaged the performance; nevertheless, he had interrupted the show three times – once when his entire music book fell onto the keys of the grand piano while Si was talking to the audience, a second time when his music light mysteriously fell onto the piano keys, and a third time when the support holding the piano lid open came loose. The giant wooden lid slammed down and then bounced twice before coming to rest. Si called an impromptu meeting where all twenty-two band members crowded into a cramped room.

"I know what you guys do," Si threatened. "If you guys don't straighten up, I will make sure you won't play in <u>any</u> other bands. And, I don't mean I will call other band leaders."

Upon saying this, he stared directly at the piano player, sternly frowned, and continued, "If you are a trumpet player, you will have no lip left, and if you are a piano player, your fingers won't work anymore!"

One day later, I awoke at my hotel in Detroit, Michigan, and gazed out over Grand Circus Park. I decided to have breakfast at a diner located directly across the street. I was an early riser and I saw none of my compatriots in the lobby or on the street, so I ambled into the diner and took a booth seat by myself. A seemingly nice, albeit weatherworn lady of advanced age took my order. She spoke in a significantly southern accent.

A bit later, while I was munching on toast, I saw Si Zentner walking across the street and heading towards the diner. He entered and took a stool seat at the counter. When the waitress approached Si, Si appeared to be in an unusually good mood. He tried to make friendly conversation with the woman, but something he said caused her to begin reliving the civil war. She began screaming at Si and shouting obscenities that I thought only sailors knew. Si never placed his order and he arose and hurriedly vacated the premises. I had never seen Si back down from a fight, so I knew something was amiss in the world.

When our band boarded the bus that afternoon, there was some excitement as we prepared for our next "gig" at the Detroit Yacht Club. The date had not been on our original itinerary, but was added later. The word was that Henry Ford II was holding a "coming out party" on the yacht club's lawn.

I had just taken my seat on the bus when Rod asked, "Where's the piano player?"

"I don't have any idea," I responded, and then added, "I haven't seen him all morning."

"I think Si had him bumped off," Rod commented. "The guy's clothes are still here on the bus."

I looked over to the hanging clothes rack at the rear of the bus. Sure enough, there hung the piano player's clothing. The bus pulled away from its mooring, and our band was heading for what we believed would be a night to remember.

It was the same year that Henry Ford II was chosen to drive the pace car at the Indianapolis 500. Henry was not a good choice as he started the Indy cars at only about 60 miles per hour, and this caused a massive 13-car crash in turn number one. Our entire band was sitting in the infield for the race due to the generosity of Precision Piston Rings Company. We played for Precision's after race party where their driver, Arnie Knepper, spoke. Arnie didn't seem too angry with Henry II, but when he showed his racing helmet with a tire track burned into its surface, a local reporter asked, "Didn't that hurt when the tire struck your head?"

Arnie replied, "Nope. It wasn't up there long."

I'm not sure, but I believe that Si booked the coming out party with Henry II after the race. Whatever the case, we were heading for the yacht club for a coming out party, and I really had no idea what that meant. I learned later that it was a celebration to introduce a 16-year-old relative of Mr. Ford to high society.

Darke County, Ohio, where I was born, never was known as a center of high society. In fact, I had no idea what the phrase "high society" meant. I knew it had something to do with money, but that was the limit of my knowledge on the subject. I expected to meet people who were far more sophisticated and educated than me. Surely, this would be an experience where I could better learn how to behave in my life journey.

When we arrived at the yacht club, we could not believe our eyes. Erected on the beautiful lawn were two large circus-style tents. Inlaid hardwood floors covered the lawn inside the tents. False ceilings were installed in both tents –

one of gold and one of red velvet. Thousands of miniature white Christmas tree lights were cut through the velvet ceilings. The chairs in each tent were upholstered in matching velvet. According to bystanders, the decorations alone had cost the Ford's $640,000. I was beginning to understand the words "HIGH society."

Five bands were hired to play that night, and Barbara McNair was one of the performers. The shows started at 8 p.m. and we finished the performances at 8 a.m. the next day.

It is very hard to put into words the feelings I had during that long night. To say that my feelings were different from my expectations would be a supreme understatement. Primarily, the rudest group of humanity I had ever encountered in one gathering surrounded me. Other adjectives that come to mind are offensive, discourteous, impolite, bad mannered, and boorish.

In my family, we were taught to be independent in thought and confident in knowledge, but also we were taught to show respect to all others, regardless of their station in life. The young and old I met at the coming out party were obviously not taught these same values. In fact, they acted as if they <u>owned</u> all of the performers. I was not alone in my observations. As we loaded up the bus and prepared for the trip to Chicago for the next job that same night, we compared notes on our collective experience. We all were amazed by the extravagance, but surprised by the lack of manners and sophistication.

I remember nothing about the trip to Chicago, but I do remember the bus pulling up in the rear of an old roaring 20's theater where we were greeted by two black men who began helping us unload our equipment. We were ushered through the back door and onto a large stage where we set up the music stands, plugged in the lights, and tuned up our instruments.

Our audience that night was a black political convention. We were an all-white band and racial relations in the United States were tense in 1965. In fact, I had personally walked through the streets of Dayton, Ohio, during one of the first race riots in the country. Our band was a bit tense before the curtain arose, and we all wondered what kind of a reception we would have.

When a stagehand raised the curtain, the sight was spectacular. The stage towered about eight feet above a beautifully inlaid wooden dance floor. Surrounding the dance floor was a horseshoe-shaped carpeted area covered by circular tables and populated by black men dressed in tuxedos and women dressed in lovely gowns. Exiting the rear of the dance floor was a grand stairway that led to one of the most magnificent mahogany bars that was decorated in highly polished brass that glistened in the lights. Branching off the stairway at three different elevations were two more horseshoe-shaped, table-covered areas.

There was no sound coming from the audience as we opened our show. As we began to play, many couples walked onto the dance floor and began to dance with elegance. I had played our book long enough that there was no need to read the music anymore. I observed our audience with great interest. What I saw was in stark contrast to what I had seen in Detroit. People danced or they listened while we played. They did not talk to each other. They simply danced or listened.

To a group of musicians, there is nothing better than having someone listen to that which you have created. Consequently, our band began to perform at a level that it had not achieved in the past. When a song would end, appreciative applause would erupt, but as the next song would start, dancing and listening would begin again. As the first set continued, our excitement became contagious. Eventually, it came time for a break. The curtain dropped and our hosts asked if we would like to join the audience. When we left the bandstand, we were greeted as if we were long lost family members who finally made it home to a reunion.

As it is written, "All good things must come to an end." We were not alone when we began to take down the equipment. Various fans in tuxedos came to our assistance. We answered their many questions, and soon we were packed up and on the road to our hotel. I felt much the same as if I were leaving home on a long journey.

-30-

Whenever I think about these two nights, I am awestruck with the contradiction in expectations. Where I expected to find sophistication and understanding, I found contempt, rudeness and rejection. Where I expected to find anger and frustration, I found kindness, wisdom and acceptance. Lessons like this alter your perceptions of life, and teach what truly is important. It is not a matter of black and white. It is a matter of humanity and elitism.

Oh yes, let us not forget the missing piano player. He never returned to our band, and at the time, no member of our band knew what happened to him. However, about seven years later, my wife and I were sitting in a restaurant in Dayton, Ohio, when I recognized a man's face within a party of diners sitting nearby, but I had no idea how I knew that face. When I looked at the man, my mind saw a piano. Every time I looked at him, I saw a piano. I walked to his table, looked down and stated, "PIANO!"

The stranger looked up and shouted, "BASS!"

It was our missing piano man.

"What happened to you?" I asked.

"When Zentner gave that speech in the closet at I.U., I thought it was a good time to get out. Especially, since we had played for that Mafia Convention in Chicago just a few days before."

I was pleased to learn that he had survived the ordeal.

Story #62: The 2,000-Pound Duck

It was back on the bus for the most arduous trek in our cross-country adventure. We headed west out of Chicago and played the next night in Lincoln, Nebraska. Next, we played in Denver, Colorado, then Reno, Nevada, and the next night we opened a one-month stand at Harvey's Wagon Wheel, located on the south shore of Lake Tahoe. Each night we were to play three one-hour shows with Barbara McNair.

The south shore of Lake Tahoe was divided into two geographic areas: (1) the California side where all of the hotels and motels were concentrated, and (2) the Nevada side where gambling was legal and casinos sprung up like cactus. Two of my fellow band members and I jointly rented a four-room suite in the Desert Inn Motel on the California side of the divide.

Staying in one place for a month was always a dream comes true, but playing in the high country of Nevada was heaven on earth for a young outdoorsman like me. Since our shows began at 9 p.m. and ended at 2 a.m., the daylight hours were completely free for any activity. I immediately went to a local stable and purchased a good horse in order to ride in the mountains. My horse was a Standard Bred/Arabian cross, which was ideal for good windedness at the high elevations.

One month seems like a short time to have a feeling of permanence, but after doing one-night stands for months on end, a month at one location felt more like a year. Our band was playing on a professional level that I had never experienced, and have not experienced since. We were like one wonderful organism where every component part knew exactly what every other component part was doing. At times, this feeling was so strong that you felt as if you were flying. The feeling was infectious to the point that our audiences would lean forward in their chairs as the band played.

Each night our popular big band would play a high-powered one-half hour show, then we would introduce our star attraction Barbara, and we would back her up for another half hour. Since the audience would change after each show, we would take a half-hour break and then play a second set, followed another half-hour later by a third set. Since I was too young to gamble legally, I spent the first four nights talking with the casino guards until they became familiar with my presence and my association with the band. They eventually assumed I was of adequate age to frequent the slot machines and other activities, which I gratefully did.

What a life! During the day, I rode my horse freely through the Ponderosa Pines in the high mountains, and then every night I was allowed to spend three hours with one of the most beautiful, gracious and talented women on earth. The between times were occupied by eating and limited gambling.

Barbara McNair had a stage presence that was electrifying. When she spoke, grown men and young boys like me would melt. Her singing voice was beautiful; however, her speaking voice had a softness and warmth like none I had ever heard. When she would introduce her signature song, "The Shadow of Your Smile," it would affect me in the same way show after show and night after night. I wanted to run off the bandstand, drag her out of the building, saddle two horses and then head for the mountains. Needless to say, those cards were never dealt, and I am sure her husband would not have approved.

Being a string bass player had its advantages. Since there is only one to a big band, I got soloist pay that was significantly better than that of a 2nd chair sax or trumpet player. Another advantage was that I had a microphone aimed at my bass on the bandstand at Harvey's.

LOVELY BARBARA McNAIR
. . .in Harvey's Pavilion

McNair Unexcelled

Barbara McNair, as Harvey's Resort Hotel patrons know, is unexcelled in putting a song across to an audience. She proved this at the Academy Award show when she presented the winning title "Shadow Of Your Smile" in a manner that convinced the movie world's celebrities that her "number" was entitled to win. Miss McNair drew one of the strongest bursts of applause throughout the show.

"Here is one of the most exciting new stars packed into an attractive frame," Emcee Bob Hope announced as he introduced the Academy Award winning song to be done by Miss McNair. It was done with style, grace and poise by Barbara, who proved that the song, and herself, were both in the winning category.

As well as she performed during the Academy Award show, Miss McNair was able to demonstrate only one of the many sides of her talent. Catching her show at Harvey's Pavilion of the Stars, July 1 through July 14, will reveal other sides to her dazzling stage appearance.

A lovely creature, Miss McNair bursts into center stage with eyes flashing, teeth sparkling and swings right into a swinging version of "Nothing Can Stop Me Now." With precise diction that makes every word count, she puts across her best two numbers, "Alley Cat" and "Sweet William Now."

Turning away from the straight performance, Miss McNair shows an unexpected ability to imitate some of the better known stage personalities: Pearl Bailey, Eartha Kitt, Jackie Mason and Carol Channing. To wrap up the sterling performance, she breaks into a "spiritual beat" and sings a lengthy and swinging medley that ends with "When The Saints Go Marching In" and brings the show closed and leaves the customers applauding for more.

Preparing the way nightly for Miss McNair is an old friend Si Zentner, who teamed up with Barbara last year during their Pavilion performances. Si Zentner warms up the audience with a selection of his unique orchestral arrangements such as "Watermelon Man," "Japanese Sandman," "On The Road To Mandalay," and a medley of one big hit, "Up The Lazy River."

Si Zentner is recognized as the creator of the newest and most successful recent sound in the big band business. His young musicians bring a crisp style and surprising variety to their performance with five saxophones, four trombones, including the mellifluous tones of Si Zentner's trombone, four trumpets and a minimum of percussion. They can swing lightly or unleash the power of the full brass section in crescendo. Either way, it's a treat to hear an honest-to-goodness big band working in the modern music idiom.

Early dining and dancing at the famous Top of the Wheel with Lenny Herman and his Orchestra, alternating with Ron Rose from 8 p.m. until 2 a.m. Late-late dining and dancing in the new Place Upstairs with pianist Joe Bushkin at the keyboard from 12:30 a.m. until 6 a.m. In the Theatre Lounge: the International IV, June 16 through July 6; Louis Jordan & the Tympany Five, June 16 through July 6; Cathy Ryan, June 18 through July 10; Gil & Nikki, June 24 through July 14; Jerry Sun June 25 through July 10; and the Waikikians, June 28 through July 7.

After about three weeks of hearing Barbara announce her signature song, I could take it no longer. During the second show one night, as Barbara prepared to say the magic words, I quietly lifted the microphone from its stand. As the final word softly left her lips, I used my favorite Donald Duck voice to squawk, "Oh, that's beauuuutiful!" It truly sounded like Walt Disney had created a 2,000-pound duck for the occasion, and nobody on stage or in the audience knew from whence the voice came.

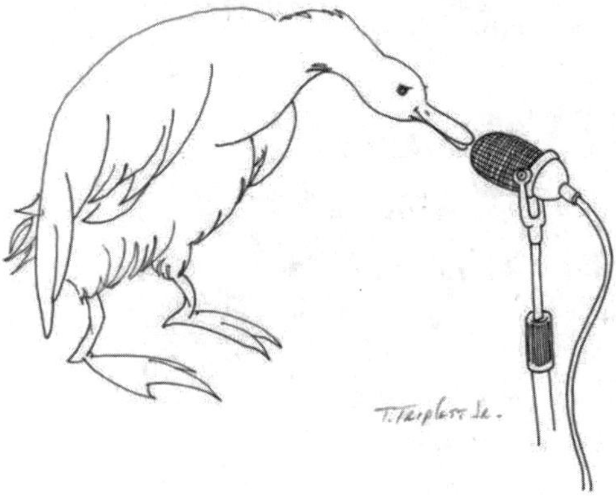

Barbara began to laugh and tears started to stream from her eyes. She tried to regain her composure and start singing, but each time she tried, she would begin to giggle again. At first, Si Zentner looked angry, but soon he too was laughing, as was the entire audience and the band members. For about a minute, time seemed to stand still. Eventually, Barbara regained her composure, and the show continued.

As we all gathered back stage, I saw Barbara questioning various band members. Suddenly, she looked directly at me and headed my way with determination.

"Are you the duck?" she asked with a serious look on her face.

Stealing a line from my friend Rod, I casually said, "I cannot tell a lie, it was I."

Barbara stared at me for a few seconds and then said, "Let me tell you what you are going to be doing. You are going to teach me how to talk like a duck."

With that said, she laughed and gave me a big smile. True to her words, I spent a brief amount of time teaching Barbara the art of Donald Duck speak.

-30-

I have no idea where I found the courage to do what I did that night. However, the brashness of my act did not hold a candle to the boldness of the lead trumpet player who played with Hank Mancini's band. Hank's band was playing at the new Harrah's on the south shore. When our band had a day off, we would go listen to another big band if one was in town. You might call it professional courtesy. We caught Hank's band one night and following the gig, several of us returned to our suite at the Desert Inn Motel.

Story #63: This is God

It was a warm August night as eight musicians headed from Harrah's to our three-man suite at the Desert Inn Motel. In the year 1965, big bands were near the end of their popularity. Consequently, the community of road musicians was very small and most musicians had friends on other bands. Such was the case as our trio hosted five members of Mancini's band for a night of story telling.

It was about three o'clock in the morning when Mancini's lead trumpet player (who will remain unnamed for reasons soon explained) walked out on our second-story balcony for a breath of fresh air.

"Hey you guys," he barked, "Come out here, quick!"

Our tiny balcony only measured about four feet in width and seven feet in length. So, it was a bit crowded as the eight of us crammed onto the appendage. It is important at this point to explain that the Desert Inn Motel was L-shaped and that our room was located in the corner of the "L." The room located on the adjacent corner of the "L" also had a balcony with twin-glass sliding doors like ours. It also would be good to explain that most of the card dealers in the Tahoe casinos at that time were female college students from UCLA or USC.

The trumpet player excitedly pointed at the glass-sliding doors in the adjacent room and said, "Look at that!"

If you are embarrassed easily, you may want to jump to the next story at this time.

Eight guys in unison focused on the well lit room behind the sliding glass doors. There, in full view, was a bedroom. On the bed was a nude old man of perhaps 65 years, and a very young and equally nude woman.

Suddenly, the trumpet player pushed us aside, ran back into our room, and then dashed out into the hallway. We could hear him running down the hall until the sound faded away.

"Where in the hell is he going?" one of the guys said.

"Hey, that girl is one of the dealers from Harrah's," another player stated. "God, I hope she's not his girl friend."

We all stared at the bedroom across the way, fully expecting the door to be kicked in by an irate trumpet player. However, nothing happened. Then we heard the sound of footsteps charging down the hallway. Our door burst open and the out-of-breath trumpet player ran back into the room, grabbed the telephone and pushed his way back onto our balcony.

The trumpet player had run down the hallway to determine the number of the room where adultery was being planned. The trumpet player called the front desk and calmly stated, "Ring room 224 please."

As our group eagerly watched, the old man in the room rolled off the bed and placed the telephone next to his ear. The trumpet player held his phone far from his mouth and in a very deep voice announced, **"THIS IS GOD! AREN'T YOU ASHAMED OF YOURSELF?"**

The old man slowly placed his phone back into its cradle, then walked back to the bed where he could be seen saying a few words to the young dealer. After a few seconds, they put on their clothing, and the old man packed his bags and left.

-30-

Following our stay at Tahoe, we headed for Los Angeles to play the last bookings for the Si Zentner Orchestra. It was the last Zentner road band to tour the country. When we disbanded in L.A., emotions were mixed for all. It was a special time in history as it marked the most massive airline strike ever seen in the United States, and very few commercial airlines were flying. Since Ray Fay had to return his bus to Chicago, I had a sure ride to the Windy City; however, getting back to Ohio would be another story.

Story #64: The Flight Home

It was early evening when as Ray and I rolled into Chicago in the road bus. It was a great trip back as Ray and I had the bus to ourselves.

"You might as well stay at my place tonight," Ray offered. "I think I can get you a flight back to Dayton in the morning," he added.

"How are you gonna do that, with the strike going on," I questioned.

"I got friends down there. Let me make a few calls," he said.

We arrived at Ray's home late that evening, and a short time later Ray came back to my room and said, "I got you and your bass booked. I'll take you to the airport in the morning."

Midway Airport looked deserted when Ray and I arrived. When I reached the gate, there were about 20 people huddled around the door. When I looked out the window, I was surprised to see a tail-dragging, twin-engine DC-3 sitting on the tarmac. The thin aluminum skin sagged and bagged over the internal ribs in the fuselage.

The ground crew ushered me to the ramp first in order that my bass could be loaded into the aisle seat at the front bulkhead. I strapped the bass in position and then buckled myself into the window seat that overlooked the starboard engine.

Everything seemed right with the world. That is until a middle-aged woman appeared in the aisle. First, she stared at my bass, and then at me, showing a look of total indignation.

"What's going on here?" she shouted at the stewardess. "There are thousands of people trying to get airplane flights and you are letting this thing take up a seat," she continued.

The stewardess calmly replied, "Listen, that thing you are pointing at paid more for its ticket than you did for yours.

With a loud "harrumph", the woman marched down the aisle and disappeared into a rear seat.

"Sheesh, I hope this is not an omen of things to come," I thought.

The plane was taxied to the runway, and then it began accelerating. First, the tail wheel lifted off the pavement, and then the old bird gracefully climbed skyward. As I watched Chicago appear in great splendor below, I thought about the contrast of the DC-3 that was carrying me home to the sleek Boeing 707 that had flown me to Las Vegas so many months earlier.

I was no longer a famous jazz musician, and like the DC-3, the music I so loved was rapidly becoming outdated. Instead of being replaced by something new and sleek, big bands were being replaced by a more primitive music that relied on showmanship but required less talent and musicianship. Even worse, I had money but no job. And, this time there was no newspaper publisher on the same plane as there was when I returned from my Air Force career.

As I stared thoughtlessly out the window, I was surprised to see the propeller on the starboard engine feather out and come to a stop. Since my father had been a research engineer on aircraft propeller actuators, I had an excellent understanding about what was happening. Then, the pitch was put back into the prop, and the blade began to rotate slowly for a few seconds before being feathered a second time. Again, its rotation ground to a stop. This sequence was repeated about five times, and still no announcement came over the speaker or from the stewardess.

Time seemed to stand very still for what felt like hours. Finally, the pilot calmly announced over the public address system, "Ladies and gentlemen, we are having some minor engine difficulties. We will be landing a little early."

"Little problem!" I thought. "The engine isn't running! And, how are we landing a little early?" A better question would be, "Where are we landing? -- in a cornfield or worse, perhaps."

It was at this point in my thoughts that the pilot interrupted with, "We will be landing in Indianapolis to correct the engine problem."

We gradually lost altitude, but the pilot made an uneventful landing in Indianapolis. He taxied the plane straight to the terminal. All of the passengers were ushered from the DC-3 and into a waiting area. We could see the DC-3 through a large glass window. The pilot guided the plane about 200 yards away from the terminal, and then he attempted to restart the failed engine. After cranking the engine for several minutes, dark black clouds began to stream from the engine. We could hear several rifle-like sounds as the engine backfired to life. The pilot advanced and retarded the throttle of the failed engine. Then, he taxied back to the terminal for boarding.

All but three of the passenger elected to find different transport to Dayton, but my bass was still strapped to the bulkhead seat, and I figured that if the pilot was crazy enough to fly, I was crazy enough to fly with him.

The takeoff from Indianapolis was uneventful, but I did notice that the plane climbed only to about 1,500 feet of altitude and we flew directly over Interstate #40 (the Old National Highway) all of the way from Indianapolis to Dayton. I clearly remember seeing about 100 bright yellow school buses parked at the bus factory in Richmond, Indiana, as we sputtered overhead.

It felt good when I reached the old homestead in Fort Jefferson. Things had not changed much there, but I had changed, and it was virtually impossible for me to explain how I had changed. I had become a professional who had performed at a very professional level with professionals. It was a feeling that I hoped to experience at some future time, but I had no idea whether I would ever have such feelings again.

-30-

Another chapter in my book of life had prematurely closed. I had returned to rural America and had no immediate plans for my future. I moved back into the family home, and, you guessed it, took a job in a gasoline filling station in Greenville. What else would you expect a jazz musician to do?

I was working at this gas station one day when the pressman with whom I worked at the Greenville Daily Advocate stopped in for a fill-up. I hadn't seen Phil North for some time, and it was good to see a familiar face.

"Hey, are you still looking for a job," he asked.

"Yes," I said, "but I have no idea what I want to do."

"I have been helping out at a newspaper in Sturgis, Michigan, when their pressman goes on vacation," he explained. "They are looking for a sports editor."

"Who would I contact?" I asked.

"The publishers name is Harold Pringle," he offered.

Phil filled me in on the details of the job, and I thanked him for the information.

I scheduled an appointment with Mr. Harold Pringle, of the Sturgis Journal, drove north, and three days later, I was the newest full-time journalist in southern Michigan. A new chapter in my life was about to be written.

Collection #4:

Canvas: Sturgis, Michigan – New Home

Setting: 1965-1969, Sturgis is a small city of about 11,000 inhabitants situated near the southern border of Michigan. The political center of the town was the Sturgis Daily Journal, a privately owned daily newspaper that was proudly printed on a very old letterpress.

The financial heart of the city was Kirsch Company, a privately held corporation that produced curtain rods and accessories. The Kirsch Company was founded by Charles W. Kirsch in 1907 after he invented the flat curtain rod. In 1960, Kirsch decorative traverse rods were introduced to the nation on national television's "The Today Show." The airport runway in Sturgis had to be lengthened to allow the Kirsch business jet to land there.

Sturgis at this time was conservative, and it had a decorative mayor supported by a professional city manager and a typical city council. Full-time police and fire departments protected its citizens in a professional manner.

Sturgis sits on U.S.-12 in St. Joseph County, a sandy place where a person cannot stand any farther than one-half mile away from a lake or stream. Residents here are proud to tell you, "If you don't like the weather here, wait a minute."

The county seat for St. Joseph County is Centreville, and it is even smaller than Sturgis. Centreville is located in the center of the county and is known for having its "r" and "e" reversed.

A State Police post was located about 12 miles west of Sturgis on U.S.-12 in a small village called White Pigeon. White Pigeon was named after an Indian chief – Wahbememe - who ran all the way from Detroit to White Pigeon to warn the white settlers of an anticipated Indian attack, then promptly dropped dead from exhaustion.

Hunting and fishing were considered national pastimes and life was good. Even though Indiana is located just a few miles south of Sturgis, Hoosiers were considered foreigners and were not to be trusted, especially during high school basketball games.

Chapter #13: Back to the Future

When I first arrived in Sturgis, the publisher – Harold Pringle – instructed me to live within the city. "The newspaper is a part of the city," Harold explained, "and, you are a part of my newspaper; therefore, you must be a part of this city also. I'll give you three days to find a place."

Harold was crowned with white hair, and he looked very distinguished. I had met others in my life that "looked" distinguished, but were not. Harold was different. He was the real deal – and honest and honorable man. I did not know that on the first day, but over time, he proved that both his heart and mind were centered in the right places.

I patrolled the town in my 1963 Volkswagen beetle, quickly located a furnished second-story apartment above the living quarters of Nicholae and Trudy Ramneantzu. Nick had been a Rumanian politician before immigrating to the United States. Trudy was Swiss born and an avid Jehovah Witness. Nick, on the other hand, was a practicing agnostic. Regardless of their different religious perspectives, they were deeply in love and inseparable.

Trudy gave me a guided tour of the second-story apartment that was impeccably clean, and Trudy made it very clear that she expected me to keep it in proper order. When we returned downstairs, Nick gave me a tour through his wonderful garden, the centerpiece of which was a colorful rose paradise.

"My goal is to create a black rose," Nick explained. "No one has ever done that."

I carried my limited wardrobe over the short walk and up the concrete steps to the front entrance, then up the staircase to my first apartment. Up until that very moment, I had always bunked in a single room with two brothers or a low-cost hotel room with fellow band members. After putting my clothing away, I sat down on the couch in my living room and gazed out the front window. "God, I thought. I finally have a home all to myself." It was great feeling.

Story #65: First Day at Work

Working for a daily newspaper in a small community can be a labor of love. For most of the editorial staff, the day began at 6 A.M., and by 4 P.M. the day's work was being published on a giant German letterpress located in the basement of our Chicago Road office.

Chicago Road in the 1920's and 30's was the primary highway that connected Chicago to Detroit. Gangsters were known to have routinely traveled the route, and at times, they dumped weapons and bodies in St. Joseph County's numerous lakes that were sprinkled along both sides of the roadway.

Entering the Sturgis Journal building, I was intrigued by how unusual it was that I was now a sports editor. I really was never involved in organized sports at Greenville High School. Yes, I loved football, and lord knows that my brothers and I tried to kill each other in our back yard games. I always found watching baseball extremely boring, and golf was very frustrating. Basketball was a thing that other farm boys and I did in area barns. Tennis obviously was a sport for girls, not real men. I did like playing horseshoes, but Sturgis was not a Mecca for pitchers. Track and field was interesting, but I knew little about the rules. Obviously, I was perfectly qualified to be a newspaper sports writer and editor.

During my brief job interview, there was not enough time available to meet the staff. So walking into the back door for the first time that morning was somewhat frightening. When I opened the door, I faced a choice of walking up the stairs to my new typewriter or down the stairs to the pressroom. More light could be seen looking down, so down the stairs I trudged. Two men, who were working on the ancient cast iron press, greeted me.

"Good morning," I said. "My name's Bill Light. I'm the new sports editor."

The slightly balding, older gentleman extended his hand and said, "Glad to meet you, Bill. I hear you came from Greenville, Ohio. So did I. My name's Pat Hunt. I'm the chief pressman, and that ugly guy over there is Al."

Al walked over and shook my hand, but never said a word. For the next several minutes, we talked over how small of a world it was and how strange it was that Pat and I came from the same small town.

The basement pressroom was a magical place. Besides the marvelous press, a large ceramic vat was simmering with a brew of lead and tin used to cast the heavy impression cylinders that were loaded onto the press. There the cylinders would pick up ink and transfer it to giant, unfurling rolls of paper at a break-neck speed. The aroma of burnt acetate emanated from a scanograver that converted a photographic image into a maze of dots on a plastic sheet. Later, the sheet would be attached to the impression cylinder via double-faced tape. Things clicked, clattered, whirred and groaned in a kind of mechanical symphony that was mesmerizing.

Pat was a wonderful host as he explained the function of every piece of equipment in detail. He was clearly the master of his world, but more importantly, he seemed genuinely interested in my opinions and me. Without suggestion, Pat offered, "Let me show you around." Up the stairs we went, into the heart of the living, breathing organism known as the Sturgis Daily Journal.

People were everywhere and traveling in all directions at the same time. It reminded me of the Zimmer's family reunions where adults and children intermingled in some mystical dance that appeared chaotic, but clearly had some grand purpose. Pat introduced me to every living soul, and each took several minutes to explain who they were and what they did.

There was Doug and Rosemary and Alice and

Carol and Mary and Marjory and Warren and Scott and Marv and George and Faye and Clara and Edith and Larry and so on and so on, and more. It was a dizzying array of names and faces, and Pat knew them all, right down to their stations in life and family heritages.

Rosemary was the daughter of a local bank president and had two children. Her husband was schizophrenic, and the couple no longer lived together. Marjory was the society editor who had held the first nail when the Journal was constructed so many years ago. She knew every living soul in Sturgis and across the border in Indiana. Mary was young and lovely, and some outsider from the county seat in Centreville was courting her.

Alice was rock solid in disposition and skill, as long as you didn't sneak up behind her and whisper in her ear, "Hello Alice." If you did, she would shriek at the top of her voice, and everyone in the plant would laugh. Warren was the janitor and he always was at work at least an hour before everyone else, unless someone like me was working at his or her typewriter throughout the night. Doug was the dapper managing editor who had a gift with words and women. Carol, who lived in a village named after the Burr Oak tree, was the passion of the editorial staff and had a marvelous way of capturing the spirit of the story. Marv

was the outgoing sports editor that I was about to replace. He was my mentor for two weeks before he headed to his new job at the daily newspaper in Three Rivers, located on the western side of the county. Faye and Clara operated two of the line-o-type machines that converted typewriter strokes into reverse-ordered lines of lead type. Larry and George assembled the lead output of Faye and Clara's work into the "turtles," -- large, flat, steel tables with side and top rails that organized the lead lines of type into pages of copy. Edith was the Journal's proofreader. She had to read each and every word that went into each and every newspaper, to insure that a poor typist like me did not end up looking like a fool. Scott ran the advertising group that generated the revenue that allowed the newspaper to exist.

Finally, I was ushered into the editorial office area, where I was introduced to my very own desk, my very own typewriter, my very own telephone, and, most importantly, my very own chair. Just as I was about to take my seat, Marv said, "Let's go, Light - we gotta cover the city beat. You're driving."

"City beat," I thought. "I'm supposed to be the sports editor."

We hopped into the VW and it was off to city hall where I met policemen, firemen and politicians. (For those of you hell bent for political correctness, there were no policewomen or firewomen in Sturgis at that time.). I was shown where to find the daily reports and where not to look. Then, it was back to the VW and on to Sturgis High School. There I met Sturgis High School Athletic Director Dick Maher, football and tennis coach Harley Pierce, and a few other lesser notables.

For a person like me who remembers every number he has ever seen, but cannot remember names to save his life, it was a very stressful day. When I returned home to my elevated abode, I studied all of the names I had recorded and tried to write physical characteristic beside the names so I would have some idea who I would face the next day.

-30-

Sturgis, Michigan, was a clean-cut town, so I felt very comfortable in my new surroundings. Some of the names mentioned in the last story will surface a few more times as the stories continue. It is hard to put into the words how I felt and feel about the members of my extended family that grew as the years passed. Most have passed on, but they will live on in my memories, and I hope to see them again on the other side, so we can catch up on the stories.

Story #66: The Inherited Curse

I had only worked at the Journal for a few weeks, when, unexpectedly, Rosemary summoned me to publisher Pringle's office to attend an impromptu editorial staff meeting.

"Wow!" I thought. "I must have really impressed everyone to be invited to a high-level staff meeting."

Since I responded quickly to Rosemary's request, I was somewhat surprised to see everyone else already present and seated.

"Make yourself at home," Harold offered.

Then Doug spoke up. "Bill," he said, "we have a long-standing tradition here at the Sturgis Journal. Marv was the torchbearer for this tradition for many years. Since you have replaced Marv, we thought it only fitting for you to carry on the tradition." Everyone smiled and nodded in agreement.

I know I should have felt honored, but in reality, I had a sense of foreboding. "Foreboding" may be too strong a word here. My memory says it was more of a suspicious feeling. I suspect it was the same feeling a convicted felon gets just before the lever to the gallows door drops open.

"What is this tradition?" I asked.

Rosemary chimed in. "You see Bill, for as long as anyone can remember, the Journal has always published a front page April Fools' Day story on or about April 1st. People in the community really look forward to it." Everyone in the room again nodded in agreement.

Doug added, "Last year Marv took a cup, turned it upside down, and then glued it onto a saucer. He painted a few black circles around the side of the cup, and then he glued a fine black thread to the bottom of the cup, which was now facing up. He took his camera and the cup and saucer to the roof of the Journal building, and then he tied the thread to an antenna rod. By positioning his camera just right, he took a picture that made the cup and saucer look just like it was hovering over Chicago Road."

Rosemary butted in, "Marv wrote a caption for the picture that said police had spotted a flying saucer circling over the city and that he had taken the picture of it. We printed the picture and caption on page one.

I felt a sense of relief. Heck, I grew up with two older brothers and had a younger sister, and all of us appreciated a good practical joke. My grandfather even founded the Greenville Chapter of the National Association of

Amalgamated Liars, and I had been a member in good standing of this fine organization for three years.

It was at about that time that Marj, the society editor, spoke up. "Last year on the day we published the flying saucer hoax, I was walking in the downtown area when an elderly lady walked up to me and said, 'Oh thank you. Thank you so much. I thought I was the only one that saw it.'"

"Are you kidding," I said.

"Really," Marj confirmed.

"What did you say?" I quizzed.

"Nothing! I just turned around and walked back to the Journal building," Marj added.

So, there it was. The staff had elected me, by a unanimous vote, the Official April Fool for the Sturgis Daily Journal. However, how could I possibly top a flying saucer made from a real cup and saucer.

My first attempt was inspired by a technology breakthrough. One day, while passing some free time in the pressroom with Pat and Al, I was studying how the Fairchild scanograver functioned. The scanograver consisted or two rotary metal drums. A photograph would be mounted on one drum, and a piece of acetate would be wrapped around the second drum. A light and a photoelectric sensor were attached to a rod that ran over the length of the photographic drum. The light beam was focused to a dot onto the surface of the photograph, and a reflection from the dot reflected back to the sensor. As the dot moved along surface of the photo, the light and dark areas in the photo were detected and the signal from the sensor was amplified, and then sent to another device that was attached a second bar that ran over the length of the second drum, where the acetate was attached and rotated. This device consisted of the vibrating needle that was surrounded by an electrical heating coil. The differences in the light intensity being reflected from the photo caused the needle to vibrate more and less, which in turn caused the needle to burn into the acetate film to different depths, proportional to the intensity of the reflected light. Consequently, a dot matrix was created in the acetate that captured a reversed image on the photo in the plastic sheet. As with all things printed in a letterpress process, the type and the image must be made backwards in order for the pictures and letter characters to be printed in the forward direction so normal human beings can read and recognize.

WARNING: I sincerely hope you are reading this story with intensity. There will be a test to insure that you have understood the function of the scanograver. I will expect you to score at least 82.7% to receive a passing grade.

Let's see if we can make this easier for the technically challenged. The scanograver copies photos on plastic. That ought to do it.

After a bit of study, it struck me that I could add one switch to the device and change the direction that one drum was scanned. Being an outdoorsman, I always shot photos of hunters and anglers with their prize catches. I had a wonderful photo of a man holding a 15-pound Northern pike. The man was looking straight into my camera lens when the photo was taken, and with both hands, he was supporting the pike in a horizontal position.

I modified the scanograver, and then I attached the picture to the photo drum. I used a magnifying glass to study the photo as it was being scanned. When the point of light illuminated the exact middle of the man's nose, I threw the switch. Voila! I had the perfect image in plastic of a man holding a Northern Pike with a head at each end.

Writing the front page story for April 1st that year was fun. Everything was tongue in cheek. For example, the fisherman's name became Bob Berdown (get it – bobber down). People in the community seemed to enjoy the spoof; however, the biggest surprise came six months later when we received a letter from a man in Florida.

"Dear sports editor," the letter began. "I need your help to settle a $50 bet I made with a friend here in Florida. I was in your town earlier this year and I saw a picture and article which showed a man who caught a two-headed fish. My friend doesn't believe such a fish could live; so, I would like a copy of the paper so I can win my bet. Thanks."

It seemed a little strange to me that anyone could believe that a fish with no waste disposal system could survive for one day, let alone 8 or 10 years.

One year, Mr. Pringle summoned me to his office. "Bill," he said, "This year why don't you come up with an April Fools story that is a little more realistic."

Looking back, asking me to write a more realistic joke probably was not the best idea Mr. Pringle ever had. Let's face it, asking me to embellish a practical joke would be akin to asking Alfred Nobel if he could make a better noisemaker for a party. In both cases, you are playing with dynamite.

Where the idea came from is beyond the limits of my memory, but airplane hijackings were popular in the late 1960's, so that seemed like a logical place to begin. Unlike today, most of the hijackings occurred when Cubans wanted to take a joy ride back to their homeland. Our airliners would fly to Cuba, let the hijackers out, and then return home.

The City had expanded Kirsch Municipal Airport just enough to allow the Kirsch Company private jet to land – sometimes not so safely. In fact, on one occasion during a light snowstorm, the Kirsch pilot misjudged the beginning of the runway, and the two landing gears were jammed through the wings. The jet skidded down the runway like a runaway bobsled, and then slid off the runway and into the grass where it finally came to rest. It was a miracle that the plane did not burst into flames. No one was hurt.

The idea of a commercial jet like a Boeing 707 landing at Kirsch Municipal Airport seemed ridiculous, but just the thought of hijackers forcing a giant airplane to land at the miniature airport seemed very humorous to me at the time.

I went to the local hobby shop, purchased a plastic model kit of a Pan Am 707 airliner, and did my best to make it look realistic during the assembly. A good friend owned a photographic studio in the downtown area, and he allowed me to use his rollout black background paper to serve as backdrop for my photo. My goal was to superimpose the photo of the model onto the tarmac at the airfield; consequently, I took my camera, equipped with a wide-angle lens, to the airfield and shot a photo. It is important to note, that there was a light snow on the ground the morning I took the photo.

Mr. Pringle had allowed me to build a photo lab in the basement of the Journal, so I spent several tedious nights perfecting a technique that allowed the model airplane to appear as a full-sized craft sitting on the field. I even dodged in fake tire tracks through the snow. Next, it was a matter of bribing one of our local policemen and two of our long-haired, teenage newspaper delivery boys to fake an arrest scene. The two boys were placed in the rear seat of the cruiser, looking away from the camera, and the officer was leaning in and applying handcuffs to one of the boy's wrists.

The story written to support the images was rather lengthy. It explained how two hapless hippies had run out of money in an eastern state, and then decided the only way to get home was to hijack a commercial airliner. The story had the airplane make a miraculous and safe landing at Kirsch Field, and local police arrested both hippies without incident or injury. The police chief was quoted in the last sentence of the fictitious story saying, "It will take some darned April Fool to get this plane back out of here."

Then, all I had to do was wait.

April 1st that year fell on a Saturday, and Saturday was a day when we arrived early to work and usually had the press cranking our newspapers by about noon. When I awoke that day, I noticed that a light late-season snow squaw had covered the ground with a thin blanket of white –

precisely the same way it did the morning the airport photo was taken. The morning was uneventful and I drove home to enjoy a nice afternoon of rest.

Drama Unfolds At Kirsch Airport

By W. C. "Bill" Light
Journal Staffwriter

Kirsch Municipal Airport entered the jumbo-sized jet age a little ahead of schedule, early Saturday morning, when a skyjacked Pan American Boeing 707 was forced to land at this undersized local facility.

The unusual chain of events started at about 7:35 A.M., today, when Kirsch Municipal Airport officials received an urgent message from the pilot of the big Pan Am jet over the airport's unicom (radio).

According to airport manager Bad Landing, the pilot explained that "a couple of nuts" had commandeered his craft in Atlanta, Ga., and had ordered him to fly to Canada. The plane developed serious engine trouble, but the hijackers would not allow the pilot to land at a major airport facility.

"We have to get this thing down," the pilot explained. "Oil is leaking all over the outside port engine. It's a definite fire hazard and we have 137 passengers aboard."

Landing immediately notified the Sturgis Fire Department and the local ambulance service who responded by sending three fire fighting units and two ambulances to the scene. Firemen stationed themselves at the southwest end of the runway in case the giant bird would be unable to stop.

Flyers Appear

Within five minutes after the pilot radioed the Sturgis airport, a silvery object appeared in the northern skyline. All eyes strained as the speck grew larger. Much to everyone's surprise the speck turned out to be a helicopter which was heading for the airport at a very high rate of speed. Within a few seconds the helicopter hovered over the airport's parking area and landed. Four dark-suited men, who identified themselves as FBI agents from the Kalamazoo and Battle Creek offices, stepped out. They apparently had been notified of the skyjacking by the Atlanta, Ga., bureau.

The FBI agents had only a few brief minutes to discuss plans with Sturgis policemen when they were interrupted by a second message from the Pan Am pilot.

"This is Pan Am flight 41. We are only four minutes out and we'll have to land on the first approach. Our flight recorders have been actuated."

Agents and police dashed to their cars and headed for the southwest end of the runway to join the apprehensive firemen. Minutes later the glittering jet burst into view as it skimmed over Wall Hill. It's landing gears and flaps were in down position and it seemed to wobble from side to side as it approached the east end of the short landing strip.

Hot Landing

The veteran pilot set the wing gears on the very edge of the runway and applied full brakes. The plane was engulfed in thick blue smoke as it screeched down the asphalt surface, eating up runway at an alarming rate.

With only about 900 feet of

Turn To SKYJACKING
(Page 12, Column 4)

JACKERS APPREHENDED — Two unidentified sky-...s, who commandeered an airliner in Atlanta, Ga., Saturday morning, are handcuffed by Sturgis police ...fter the large jet was forced to land at Kirsch Muni... Airport. The alleged hijackers were knocked uncon... when the plane skidded out of control on landing. The ...ers were taken to the local police department where ... being held.

EMPTIED SKYJACKED AIRLINER RESTS IN EAST FIELD AT KIRSCH MUNICIPAL AIRPORT

At two o'clock in the afternoon, the telephone interrupted my solitude.

"Hello," I said.

"Dammit Light, the next time you pull a practical joke, you damn well better get crowd control in place," Came the terse response.

"Who is this?" I asked.

Who it was, was the manager of the airport, and he was not a happy camper.

"What's going on?" I requested.

"I'll tell you what's going on," he yelled. "The whole damn town is blocked with traffic. That's what's going on."

He was correct. When I arrived on the scene, there was no way to get near the airport because cars and trucks plugged both Centreville and Chicago Roads. If anything resembled a three-ring circus, Sturgis, Michigan, did that fateful day.

I was able to get to the Journal building, and I grabbed a copy of the newspaper that I had not waited to pick up when it went to press. When I read my own story, I was shocked to see that the last paragraph of the article had been jumped to page two, due to space problems on page one. Many readers never saw the punch line. I wanted to go to the airport to shoot pictures of the throngs of people, but I figured that was not a good idea since my byline headed the story. Consequently, I decided that retreat was the better part of valor, and I returned home.

Sunday was a very, very long day. Most of the day I thought about what Monday morning might bring. Surely, Harold would not fire me since he had requested a more realistic story. On the other hand, complaints from political figures might pressure Harold to send the Ohio boy back from whence he came. Then, there was the police department that was forced to call in officers to get the traffic back under control. God, it was lonely.

Monday morning, I arrived at work earlier than usual. Warren was there ahead of me.

"That was some kind of mess here on Saturday wasn't it," Warren commented. "Boy, there were cars everywhere."

"Yeawl, it was some kind of mess," I repeated.

"Whatdaya think Harold will say?" Warren asked.

"I have no idea," I responded. "I just hope he still has a sense of humor."

I turned on the light to my office area and started working on something, but for the life of me, I have no idea what. At about 6:30 AM the phone began to ring. The first two calls I answered came as a total surprise. The first call was from a reporter from United Press International (UPI), and he wanted to know if I could tell him about the airplane hijacking that had occurred. He said he was unable to get any information from the police department. I was just about done explaining to him that it was just a joke, when ringing announced a second call. This time it was another wire service, Associated Press (AP), on the line. The AP guy also heard about the hijacking, and he was very upset that no information was forthcoming from various agencies. Again, I explained the situation.

The third call received was the most perplexing of all. The conversation went like this:

Me: "Sturgis Journal"

Voice: "Who is this speaking?"

Me: "Bill Light....Who is this speaking?"

Voice: "This is (name withheld) from the FBI bureau in Kalamazoo. What is your position there?"

Me: "Sports editor."

Voice: "Is there any chance you can tell me which of our agents was present during the Pan Am hijacking that occurred on Saturday."

I did not know whether to laugh or cry, and I certainly had reservations about answering his questions. How was it possible that the best police agency in the world would not know where its agents were? Moreover, how could it be that the FBI would only be checking into such an extreme incident nearly 40 hours after it supposedly occurred?

"God!" I thought, "I'm going to prison. I explained to the FBI officer that it was an April Fools joke that was a Sturgis Journal tradition; however, he failed to see the humor.

The remainder of Monday morning was a total blur. I fielded many calls. Some were congratulatory while others were cynical and abrasive. One elderly woman called and said, "How could you make fun of such a tragedy?"

"What tragedy?" I queried. "No one was hurt and the bad guys got caught."

"It's not funny to make fun of such a terrible thing," she continued.

At one point in the conversation, I took a defensive posture and asked, "You must not have liked Will Rogers, did you?"

"Will Rogers has nothing to do with this!" she barked, and promptly hung up the phone.

When I answered another call, the young woman on the other end was laughing and giggling.

"Can I help you?" I asked.

"Oh, thank you. Thank you very much," she said while trying to suppress more giggles. "I know you probably think I'm nuts, but you made my day." Again, she began laughing.

Her laugh was infectious, and I caught myself laughing with her, without knowing the source of her joy.

"What's so funny?" I begged.

"My husband! That's what's funny. He went up to the coffee shop beside the Journal on Saturday and was eating a donut and reading the morning paper. He came skidding into the driveway at our house and then started honking the horn. When I ran out of the house, he threw the *newspaper at me and yelled, 'Come on! There's an huge jet airplane at Kirsch.' I ran into the house to get my jacket, but when I returned, he already had left without me. When I read the article, I saw it was an April Fools' joke. He has always called me gullible. Thank you. Thank you very much."*

-30-

To this very day, I am amazed how many people were fooled by what appears to be a ridiculously obvious hoax. Such a large Boeing 707 jet could not have landed safely at Kirsch Municipal Airport. FBI officer surely would have notified their bosses had they been present when hippy hijackers were arrested. Even if the event did take place, how could it be considered a tragedy if no one was hurt and the bad guys were put to justice. I still keep an original copy of the story in my "funny file" to remind me of the wide variations in people and perception.

Story #67: My Friend Dale

On a few rare occasions, I have met someone for the first time, but have known him or her forever. Such was the case when I met Dale Randall. Dale was a specialized officer of the law. More precisely, he was a Michigan Department of Natural Resources field officer, a job he held until he retired to pursue his many avocations on a full-time basis.

Dale called his home White Pigeon -- you know, the place where the Indian ran hundreds of miles to save his white brothers, then dropped dead. White Pigeon also was the location of a State Police Post, a place where Dale frequently stopped on business or just to spend some time and share stories with the troopers stationed there.

It is very hard to describe a man like Dale. He was good at just about everything he did. He had a gentle calm about him that transcended about any tough circumstance in which he found himself. He was an avid amateur radio operator (HAM). He was an outdoorsman and a good musician in his own world that centered on bluegrass music. He could repair musical instruments, or just about anything else, that broke. He also had a vivid imagination that led him to many inventive concepts.

I was lucky to have made Dale's acquaintance in a time before political correctness and legalism ran amuck in America. This allowed me to ride along with Dale as he patrolled the highways and byways of St. Joseph and surrounding counties, seeking out those who might deliberately do injustice to wildlife or the environment in which it thrives.

There are hundreds of stories I could relate to you about my adventures with Dale; however, one story in particular stands out. It may be hard for you to believe, but Dale and I saved the entire political system of the State of Michigan from annihilation.

It all started one morning when the Dale and I met in the small diner that sat immediately to the east of the Sturgis Journal building. The diner always was crowded and noisy, but it served good coffee at a fair price, and the donuts were great. It was a gathering place for all sects of society – at least all sects of society of the male gender. Other than waitresses, I cannot remember seeing many women gathering there.

As usual, Dale and I were talking about many things, but nothing in particular. Four fishermen were sitting in the booth across from us, and occasionally the volume of their conversation peaked above ours, so it became impossible not to listen. At one point, we overheard one of the men say, "I don't know what they were thinking. How could they open bass season after the Memorial Day weekend."

For those of you non-Michiganders, this might not sound like a radical and subversive statement, but in Michigan it is pure heresy to utter words aloud that in any way would jeopardize the opening of bass season.

The opening of bass season in Michigan ranks higher that the assassination of a political figure or the start of a world war. In fact, there are those who believe that if bass season does not open at the pre-destined time, the sun will fall from the sky and crash to the earth with such a sound that all people will go deaf.

I looked at Dale and said, "That guy can't be right, can he?"

"Nah," Dale replied. "That's crazy. Bass season always opens before the Memorial Day weekend."

The conversation may have ended right then and there, but one must understand that politicians are involved in setting dates for the opening and closing of things all over the world. In addition, politicians are infamous for routinely screwing things up. Even knowing this, it was hard for Dale and me to believe that the Michigan Legislature would have enough courage to mess with the opening of bass season.

Dale pulled out his DNR calendar and checked the dates. "Oh God!" he said under his breath. "They're right."

It may not have taken on such importance, but the Memorial Day weekend was only a couple of weeks away, and the date could only be changed by a change in the law.

One of the anglers in the other booth noticed Dale's uniform. He leaned over and demanded, "Are you going to arrest us if we are fishing for bass over the Memorial Day weekend?"

Dale was seldom at a loss for words, but he really had no good answer for the man. Saying that he would not arrest people he saw fishing for bass might cost him his job; however, arresting people he saw fishing for bass might cost him his life. Being between a rock and a hard place would have been far more desirable than the predicament Dale and the DNR were in.

"Let's go back to my office," I offered in order to get Dale away from the onslaught of questions.

I sat down behind my desk and Dale seated himself in my guest chair.

"Let's call Ralph McMullen," I suggested.

"Are you crazy?" Dale asked. "I can't get through to Ralph McMullen and I work for him."

Ralph McMullen was the head of the Michigan Department of Natural Resources and probably was one of the best directors of all time. People who have never worked at the top of any profession always assume that people at the top are aware of all situations. Conspiracy theorists believe these leaders plot and plan all of the bad things that occur in the world. This, of course, is seldom true, so it was quite possible that Ralph McMullen was not aware of the catastrophic chain of events that put the opening of bass season in jeopardy.

"Let's give him a call," I told Dale. "In my experience it is always better to start at the top of the tree than starting at the bottom. Even if you fall down a bit, you will still end up higher than you would if you started at the bottom."

With that, I looked up and dialed the number for the DNR. A pleasant sounding woman answered the phone, and I said, "Hello, this is Bill Light. I am the outdoor editor for the Sturgis Daily Journal. May I please speak with Ralph McMullen?'

"One moment, Sir," came the reply.

A few seconds passed, and then a voice on the other end of the phone said, "Hello, this is Ralph McMullen, how can I help you?"

I winked at Dale and then began explaining the situation to Ralph. Ralph was flabbergasted. For fun, I asked, "Will the DNR officers be arresting people if they are caught bass fishing over the Memorial Day holidays?"

It didn't take Ralph but a few seconds to figure out what had happened. The Michigan Legislature tired of having to deal with the opening date year after year, so they picked a fixed date, but they had forgotten that the Memorial Day weekend is not a fixed date. What a mess!

Ralph promised he would do whatever he could to straighten things out, but he could not predict how the legislators would respond. I thanked Ralph and hung up the phone.

"Well Dale, are you going to arrest people or not?" I challenged while trying to keep a straight face.

We both laughed. Dale went back to work, as did I.

As you already know, I could drag this story on and on to raise the suspense level. But, for what reason? Any reader who has read this far can't be too stupid, so you have guessed the story must have a happy ending, or you would have heard of the assassination of all Michigan legislators. The truth is that the Michigan Legislature authored and passed a bill in record time, and bass season was saved.

-30-

Dale Randall and I do not see each other as much as I would like, as we are separated by time and place. He and his vivacious wife Margaret still live in White Pigeon, where Margaret has become a local political activist. When I do get the chance to stop in, it is as if time has stood still. Our common interests have not changed, and we still enjoy telling a story or two, just to stay in practice.

Both of our families have grown up and flown out of the nest. Neither of us could have predicted the course our lives have taken, but the power of the stories has helped us carry on.

Story #68: Mr. Referee, Mr. Referee

Tell me the truth. Would you ever believe a person with a first name like Harley would achieve a near god-like state? No, no........don't tell he about Harley-Davidson. Harley-Davidson was two people and the "Harley" is one's last name, not a first name.

The Harley you are about to meet was one of the most remarkable men I can remember. His full name was Harley Pierce, and I met him on my first official day of work for the Sturgis Journal. However, he did not look like your stereotypical football coach!

Harley was a quiet man who, on the surface, seemed very polite and somewhat unassuming. He had a natural charm and an innate curiosity about many subjects. He was honest and forthright, but all of these characteristics belie a drive and talent that, without question, changed the lives of hundreds, if not thousands, of America's youth in a very positive manner.

When I moved to Sturgis, Harley was the head coach of the Trojans' football and tennis programs, and he assisted with other sports as well. I always loved football, but I thought tennis was for girls and rich kids that leaned slightly left of center. All of those perceptions were about to change.

My job was to provide the community with news and stories about local athletics and other outdoor activities. Consequently, frequent visits were in order to Sturgis High School, as well as to all of the home games for a variety of sports. Talking to all of the Sturgis coaches was only part of the job that also consisted of having conversations with the county coaches, and the writing stories for all of the county games as well. This meant many long hours at my desk. On Friday nights during football season, I would shoot photos at several games and then return to the office to process the film, print the photos, collect the game results via telephone from coaches, and then write about two newspaper pages of game-story copy from 10 pm to 3:30 am. I slept across three chairs; then Warren would wake me up at 6 AM, and I would finish my work and leave for home at about 11 AM.

Of all the coaches with whom I talked and worked, Harley Pierce is the most remembered. Harley was a very special human being. Not because of his winning records, but more for the way he communicated with other human beings, regardless of age. Harley spoke in a language for which there are no words. I was never able to understand fully how Harley could have such a profound and positive effect on the lives of so many. I have met many people who seem sincere, but Harley's sincerity transcended the bounds of normal folks.

It may sound strange, but I cannot honestly remember a time when I saw Harley angry. I am sure it must have happened occasionally, but I never saw it. During a very tense football game with an archrival, the officiating was terrible at best and biased at worst. I had a strong urge to shout obscenities at the men in striped shirts, but Harley maintained a sense of calm when things were looking particularly bad for the Trojans. Then it happened. It was one of the worst calls I have ever seen an official make. Harley could not contain himself. He took two steps towards a field official, and then, in a very polite but forceful voice, said, "Mr. Referee, Mr. Referee!" Then, he returned to the bench and talked to his players. The Trojans rallied despite the bad calls, and won the day.

Before I began writing this story, I had not checked to see what happened to Harley Pierce after I left Michigan in 1972. Look at what a man of great class and knowledge can accomplish:

- In Michigan, Harley's gridders amassed a record of 386 wins against 69 losses, and won 23 regional championships and 7 Class B state crowns.
- The Trojans collected 22 conference championships in one of the toughest conferences in the state – the Twin Valley Athletic Association.
- Two of the Mid-America Conference coaches are Pierce trained men -- at Eastern Michigan University Dan Ryan heads the men's varsity and at Ball State University, Bill Richards is the successful mentor.
- In the fall of the 1969-70 academic year, Harley's football team won the Class B championship, while in the spring, his tennis team also earned the state title.

- Harley was the summer tennis director for Sturgis for 30 consecutive years.
- The Michigan High School Coaches Association installed Harley into MHSCA Hall of Fame.
- Harley was the Class 'B' Coach of the Year in 1978.
- In 1979, Harley was chosen the National Coach of the Year by the NHSACA.

What does not show up in this short list of accomplishments is the long-term goodness that Harley passed on to his countless students and those like me who watched his techniques from the sideline.

My hat's off to you Harley!

-30-

My life at age 59 is much different than it was when I met Harley Pierce. My involvement in organized sports waned for many years until my eldest son decided he liked to play football. I watched him develop from Pee Wee League, through junior high and senior high school years, then on to an All American career at Purdue University, and finally as a professional left offensive tackle for the New England Patriots. To date Matt has collected seven bowl rings, including rings from three Super Bowls. I watched with interest as Matt learned from various coaches from high school to the likes of Joe Tiller and Bill Belichick. However, from my perspective, I have met no man who personifies coaching more expertly than does Harley Pierce.

Chapter #14: The German Invasion

Story #69: Sie sind Schön

It was one of those assignments that many newspaper writer/photographers hate to get – one that consumes another evening by taking place somewhere between supper and sleep time.

Rosemary gave me the assignment. "I want you to take your camera and go over to the Sturges-Young Civic Center tonight. There is a group of young Germans arriving under the auspices of an Experiment in International Living. Get some pictures and find out what's going on."

Now, you might be thinking that I just spelled the name of the civic center and auditorium incorrectly. You would be mistaken. There really was a Sturges who lived in Sturgis. In addition, an Experiment in International Living was an organization dedicated to the idea that various peoples of the world would get along better if they could live together for a few months. Now back to the story.

When I arrived on the scene that evening, the Germans and the host families already were enjoying tea and crumpets, or some other high-society culinary nibbles. My goal was to shoot a few pictures, ask a few questions and run, but that suddenly changed when I noticed a most strikingly beautiful young woman that clearly stood out in the crowd. I weaseled my way through the assembly in the general direction of the dark-haired beauty, and just to look official, I snapped a few pictures along the way.

Most of the eight German visitors were young women ranging from 20 to 25 years of age and most spoke better English than some of their hosts. One German man also arrived. He was partially balding and wore small round glasses. He looked like a 35-year-old accountant. As it turned out, he was, and he spoke in very broken English. He was standing by himself, and his friendly smile seemed jerky as if it were trying to hide a very uncomfortable feeling.

"Hi," I said. "My name is Bill Light. I work for the local newspaper."

"My name ist Eckhard Wolf," he said quietly.

Eckhard and I tried to communicate for a few minutes, and then I pointed at the dark-haired girl and asked, "Who is she?"

"She is Gabriele Zach (pronounced Gah-bree-ãla Tsahk)," Eckhard replied. "She is to stay with the Pilkington's."

I was making progress, so I excused myself and continued towards my goal. Looking back, it is obvious that I was being much too obvious, but at the time, purpose clouded all such social vision. When Gabriele finally stood before me, her beauty was even more dramatic; however, her elegance, intellect and poise superseded her physical attributes. We talked for a few minutes, and then the party ended and the visitors joined up with their adopted families and left.

When I went to work the next day, I processed the photos, wrote some appropriate words, and submitted them to Rosemary for her perusal. Rosemary thanked me for my evening of sacrifice and complimented my story. I reciprocated by volunteering for any assignments that might involve the Experiment in International Living.

The summer with the Germans was a time in my life that will never be forgotten. Eckhard and Gabriele became my closest friends, and we spent many hours together, living and learning about different cultures.

-30-

Story #70: A Matter of Language

I did not speak or understand a word of German. My German relatives, who first immigrated to the United States, gave up their native tongues in one generation because they believed that a common language would benefit the new nation. Specifically, the parents ban their children from speaking German, not because they were ashamed of their Germanic heritage, but because they really believed that one world language would benefit understanding.

Communicating with Gabriele was easy because her use of English was better than mine. Gabriele spoke three languages fluently and another one very well. Communication with Eckhard could be painfully slow, but his English was far better than my No-German.

One day as Gabriele and I were discussing the affairs of the world, I asked, "How do you like the English language?"

"I love it," she answered, "especially in poetry. But it's strange," she added in a non-condemning manner.

"What do you mean?" I wondered.

"Well," she said, "you have so many words that mean the same thing."

"Like what?" I added.

Gabriele thought for a second and then responded, "A deer, a buck, a doe, a stag, a fawn."

This didn't seem strange to me, so I asked, "What do you call a baby deer?"

With no hesitation, Gabriele, in English, said, "A baby deer."

-30-

I must tell you that the thought of calling a fawn a baby deer had never crossed my mind. My experiences with Gabriele and Eckhard gave me a renewed thirst for language; however, I did not take the time to understand and speak the German language until business sent me to Deutschland in the 1980's.

Building trust in a relationship is always important. I have known some people with whom it was virtually impossible to develop a trusting relationship due to past baggage they carry in their minds. Eckhard Wolf was <u>not</u> one of these.

Story #71: A Matter of Trust

Gabriele, Eckhard and I spent many hours together that summer. We built a mutual trust that we all respected. At times, we would just gather at the most convenient place available and talk about whatever subject would surface.

Eckhard, I learned, had one of the gentlest spirits I had ever encountered. He had a marvelous sense of humor and an innate generosity. One day, I asked Eckhard an innocent question, and the response I received gave me a lasting faith that, even in the darkest times, we should not give up on our fellow man.

"Eckhard," I asked, "why did you decide to come to the United States for this summer visit? Didn't you have to give up your job for this long of a stay?"

Eckhard looked into my eyes as if searching for a signal that would allow him to speak from his heart. Then, in very broken English, he related the following:

"My father hated Americans. He vas in dee German SS during dee var. Vee could not speak of dee United States in our house or he veud fly into a rage. He said Americans ver dee vurst people on dee earth." Eckhard looked towards the floor.

I was speechless, which was some kind of a miracle in itself. After a stunned moment of silence I asked, "What in the world are you doing here?"

Eckhard smiled and replied, "Vell, I yust got to tinking dat ders no peoples on dee ãrth dat could be zoe bad, zoe, I decided to zee for myzelf."

I lost track of Eckhard after he returned to Germany. He told me he had a wonderful time in the United States and genuinely loved the people he met. Eckhard also left a lasting legacy in the minds of the Americans with whom he made contact, and there is seldom a week goes by that I don't think of my gentle and loving friend, whose intellect and spirit lifted him above hatred and anger.

My next two stories record two of the most bizarre experiences of my life. If you find yourself doubting the veracity, especially when you read the second story, please keep in mind that I am the farthest thing from a mystic that you could ever meet, and to this very day, I still have no rational understanding of what transpired.

Story #72: A Matter of Perspective

The relationship that developed between Gabriele and I did not have any the characteristics of a dime store romance novel. We were not lovers; we were searchers. Both of us were seeking a better understanding of the world and people around us.

Gabriele was raised in a small German town called Hückeswagen, where her father, Hans Zach, owned and operated a machine shop where he made parts for bicycles and Volkswagens. She explained to me that the town was named after a farmer whose team of horses decided to stampede, right through the middle of the town. The farmer pulled on the reins with all of his strength, and repeatedly yelled, "Hüüüü, Hüüüü!" (Pronounced "Hoo Hoo") as the wagon careened through the streets. The name of the town quite literally means, "whoa wagon."

In German families, especially those where a father owns a business, it is not unusual for a daughter to take part in the business activities. Gabriele was no exception.

"Dear Bill," she said, "I have an appointment with the Schwinn Bicycle Company in Chicago on Sunday, but I am not sure of the best way to get there. We think we might be able to make some parts for them."

"I am not doing anything special on Sunday, and I would be glad to drive you there. I must be back at work early Monday, so I will just drive back after I drop you off," I offered.

"Oh no, that's asking too much," she said as she shook her head from side to side.

I didn't say so, but at the time I could think of nothing that I would rather be doing than driving to Chicago with Gabriele Zach on a bright and sunny Sunday afternoon.

At that time, I owned an Opel GT sports car that was blueprinted in Germany before being shipped to Detroit. For those of you not familiar with the wild and crazy world of racing, having a car blueprinted means to take special care in balancing every component part in the engine and drive train to insure maximum efficiency. I used to drive to work, as well as drive it in cross country events, drag racing tracks, and circuit tracks. On the driver's door was stenciled, "Wild Willy's Wagon." Getting to Chicago from Sturgis didn't take long in my four-cylinder, 1.5 liter, cam-in-head-engine-powered machine.

When we arrived at Gabriele's hotel, I carried her bags to the room. The room was stuffy, so I put the bags in the closet and walked over to open a window to spend a few moments enjoying the view of downtown Chicago. It was getting late, so I had to get back on the road immediately. When I turned around to say my goodbyes to Gabriele, she was in the process of changing into her evening clothes; however, she was stark naked.

At that instant in time, time itself did not seem to exist, and I had mixed feelings. I didn't know whether to turn back around, make a comment, apologize, or make an advance. Gabriele, on the other hand, seemed to be in perfect control of her senses, and seemed not to be aware that I was in the room, as she continued with her dressing ballet. I never thought that watching someone putting on clothing could be an art form, but it was. The movements and form were poetic, so I simply observed like an aficionado of the Opera might do when watching the Dance of the Sugar Plum Fairies. She was magnificent.

Within a few minutes, Gabriele was ready for a night on the town with her business associates from Schwinn. I was back on the road, and heading for Sturgis - carrying a head full of visions and wonder.

The next morning, I arrived at the Journal and immediately headed to the pressroom for the morning coffee ritual with Pat and Al. Pat was my senior by 24 years, and he was wise in the ways of the world. I could talk to Pat about things I would never consider telling others.

"You won't believe what happened to me yesterday," I bragged.

"What happened?" Pat asked.

"It was crazy," I said. Then, I told Pat the story that I just related to you -- in all of its wonderful detail. I finished by saying, "I am amazed that the customs in Europe are so much different from ours. She never said a thing. She just changed her clothes right there in front of God and me, and she never said a thing."

Pat paused and then stated with authority, "Did you ever think that she might be wondering about the strange customs in the United States where a man stays in a woman's bedroom while she is changing her clothes."

-30-

I must admit that Pat's idea never crossed my mind, and I was too embarrassed to ask Gabriele which perspective was correct. Gabriele and I remained close for the remainder of her stay; however, one bizarre happening nearly ruined everything.

Story #73: Broken Trust?

It had been a long Friday night, and even a longer Saturday morning. I slept on my three favorite chairs by my office desk, and Warren shook me awake as he had on so many other occasions.

My mind wasn't focused on the tasks at hand. It was thinking about the joy of going home where I could catch a catnap before going fishing. It was about 9 AM when my phone rang. It was Gabriele.

"Dear Bill," she said, "Several of the gang are here at Pilkington's. Why don't you come over so we can plan something to do?"

It wasn't like I ever had hordes of women calling me. In fact, for a not-so-handsome guy who walked with a limp, I felt honored when any female showed interest.

"Sure, I'll be over as soon as I get out of here. It will probably be about 10:30 or so," I said.

We said our goodbyes, and true to my sleepy words, I drove to the Pilkington's house. There were three other German girls there when I arrived, and they were very busy discussing whatever it is that girls discuss. I noticed the television was on, so I sat down on the sofa and stared at the screen, and then slumped into some type of exhaustion-driven stupor. The German girls were talking about going to a picnic on Sunday, and they were to meet with some French students who were staying in LaGrange, Indiana, which is located just a few miles south of Sturgis. I listened to their planning right up to the point where they reached a transportation impasse.

I turned my head, looked at Gabriele, and then offered, "Why don't we just borrow a van from Ted Plock, and all of you can ride together." Ted was a friend who owned the local Buick dealership.

What happened next came as a total surprise. All of the German girls stared at me in a manner that suggested I was Satan personified.

"What's going on?" I asked.

"I thought you didn't speak German," Gabriele said in a very abrupt tone that I had never before heard her use. Her demeanor turned stone cold.

"I don't speak German," I said. "You know I don't speak German."

"Well, you certainly understand German," she added.

"No I don't," I barked.

"We were speaking German," she chided.

"Yeah, right," I laughed, but the Germans were not laughing. Frankly, I thought they were joking. "Gabriele," I reminded, "You know very well that I only know about two or three German words."

"Then how do you explain knowing what we were taking about?" she frowned.

"I know what you were talking about because you were speaking the King's English, and I understand the King's English very well." The words came out of my mouth in a way that told Gabriele I was getting very tired with the inquisition.

"You and I need to talk," she said emphatically.

With that, she motioned for me to follow her out of the house, and I did so without hesitation.

Gabriele and I did talk, but the trust she had in me was shaken by something that I had no way to explain. Indeed, the girls had been talking in pure German, and in all honesty, what I heard with my ears and mind was pure English. As Grandma Z used to say, "The Lord works in mysterious ways."

Never before and never again was I able to comprehend German miraculously. However, this singular event created in me a desire to learn German, at least to the degree that I would be able to communicate effectively if ever put into a similar situation. The strange happening also increased my faith, and lent credence that Pentecost may have really occurred as it is written in the Bible.

When I attended Greenville High School, I wanted to learn the German language because some of the best technical papers regarding subjects that interested me were written in German. Unfortunately, the school administration would not allow the school's qualified instructor to teach the language "because of the war." I felt at the time, and still feel, that our administration and the public at large were foolish. Later in life, while working as a licensed chemist and bacteriologist for a municipality, I used German numerical notation in my reports so that the various numbers could not be confused. My superior ordered me to stop using this notation, "because it isn't American." In other words, he was willing to risk human health for political reasons and personal feelings. I found these bigoted and uniformed attitudes destructive. Close-mindedness and a failure to recognize universal truths bring about wars, death and destruction.

I have been privileged to meet many people from many different countries who profess different beliefs and faiths, but the most dangerous of all are those with no faith.

Chapter #15: Closing Remarks

I sincerely hope you have enjoyed this book, and my wish is that the stories will help you understand how human beings might approach their relationships with others in a less destructive manner. The stories are about the broad and inclusive canvas of life. If the stories bring a little hope, joy or introspection into your life, then my goal has been reached. There are so many more stories to tell, but this book has reached its limit. Perhaps at a future time, I will find the heart and wisdom to share with you the second chapter of my life, writing the stories of those who have crossed my path and influenced my journey.

The second chapter involves marriage, and the birth and development of my children, all of whom always amazed me and never disappointed me. I would like to tell you about Monk Watson, Dr. W. Edwards Deming, and Dr. Gipsie Ranney – all masters of their fields of endeavor, who left indelible marks in my mind. Perhaps you might find it interesting to learn what it was like for a man, who never attended a day in college, to be allowed to teach at two.

Oh, how I would like to capture in words the wonder and pride I felt when my loving daughter provided me with my first granddaughter.

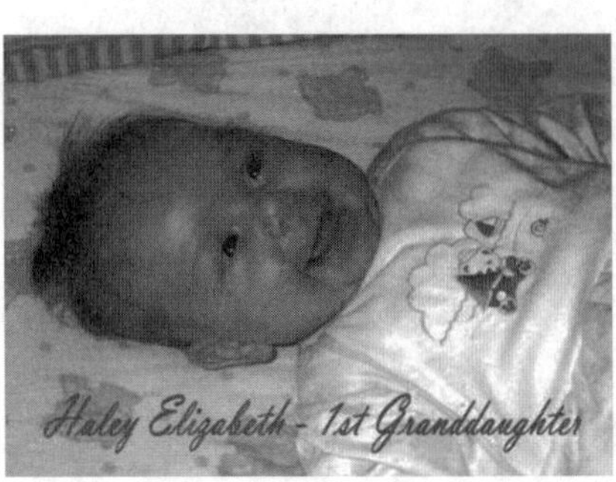

It would be fun to jot down the emotional rollercoaster ride my son, Matt, and I took as he worked his way from Pee Wee League football through four post-season college bowl games, including the Rose Bowl, and three NFL Super Bowls.

Perhaps, I will be able to give you an update on the progress of my youngest son, Mark, who is pursuing his personal dream of becoming a famous movie director and producer by attending Emerson College in Boston.

Would you, I wonder, be interested in the wonderful adventures my family and I had with Presbyterian Pastor David Layman, his lovely wife and beautiful children as we worked with children from the hill country of impoverished Eastern Kentucky.

A Log Presbyterian Church in Valley near Cow Creek, Kentucky

Traveling there by word would allow me to introduce you to Kenny who, while sitting around a campfire one night, looked me in the eyes and said, “You’re mahrreed, ain’t ya Bill?”

“Why yes Kenny, I am married,” I responded. “How did you know that?”

Kenny thought for a second and explained, “You got holes in your pants.”

“Holes in my pants!” I exclaimed, “How could you tell I was married by holes in my pants?”

Well, you shore ain’t sparkin’ no girls down here if ya got holes in your pants.”

Wisdom can be found in the most obscure places.

If -- God willing -- you have enjoyed this book, do not forget to capture your stories through the written word so they can be passed to future generations.

Thank you for caring, and in the immortal words of the world’s most loving clown, Red Skelton, “May God bless.”

There is one last story to be read. Please turn the page and enjoy.

Below is a very special story – indeed! It is written in perfect English, but **DO NOT READ IT**! Instead, give it to a friend (or enemy for that matter) and tell him or her that you forgot your glasses, and then ask him or her to read it to you aloud. Just sit back and enjoy the show. If the reader finishes the story, ask him or her to explain the meaning of the story to you.

Story #74: I Love English

By W.C. Light

Some of my families were farmers. It was their job to produce produce. Being of a scientific mind, it came to me one day that it might be possible to teach a sow to sow cedar seeds. At first the magnitude of this did not register, but later my thoughts reached a high tonal register, and I decided to register a register with the patent register. There also was no time like the present to present a present to my relatives and they did not object to the object of my desires.

Being a very regular type of guy and one who served as an army regular, I made regular trips to the barnyard to study the intelligence of the sows. Each night I would return to my study to study, and then rise each morning to stare at the cedars on the rise behind the barn and pray that a new thought would rise to the top of my mind.

Once I had selected a sow, I decided to subject the subject to a series of tests. First I spent an entire evening evening out a large expanse of dirt. To the sow, this dirt desert looked like dessert, but I had to desert this desert to find a seamstress or sewer that might help me sew a seed bag for the cedar seeds before the desert turned into a sewer. It was time for me to get the lead out and lead the sow to the sewer or seamstress. I knew that if I let the sow alone in the desert, the desert would become so full of refuse; the sewer would refuse to work for me. Besides, if the sewer were to slip in the refuse and then refuse to accept workmen's compensation, my insurance would be invalid for the invalid.

When the sow and I arrived at the home of the Polish sewer, he requested that I close the door and wait until he could polish his Polish furniture. Of course I agreed, but I was too close to the door to close it. I tried not to step on the sow, so I moved my foot onto the front step and then stumbled, cutting my hand in the process. The sewer shed a tear when he saw the tear in my hand. He became concerned when the wind would not allow him to wind a bandage around the wound. With sure determination, he wound the wound. I seem to remember that, because of the high winds, the number of winds on the wound was wound so tight, that the wound became number.

I explained to the sewer that on that very evening I had been evening out a pile of dirt where I could teach my sow to sow cedars with my new cedar seeder, and that I was about to subject my subject to a series of tests. Smiling, the sewer said, "I am glad you picked a sow to sow and not a deer because a buck does funny things when does are around."

I laughed and added, "I was going to use a dove, but it dove into the bushes."

He smiled and retorted, "I think I saw the saw you used to saw cedars for the seeder when the dove dove."

Conversations like the one above allow me to intimate that the sewer became an intimate friend.

Eventually, the sewer sewed several seeders to allow my sow to sow cedars; so my farming family didn't have to desert the dirt desert and held cedar sales to raise funds, eventually setting sail to new lands where they could produce produce thereafter.

The END